A WOMAN IN THE WILDERNESS

A WOMAN IN THE WILDERNESS

Mel Greider and Friends

Illustrator Roy Martin

New Leaf Press
Harrison, Arkansas

© by New Leaf Press, Inc. All rights reserved.
Published by New Leaf Press, Harrison, Arkansas,

Printed in the United States of America.

Library of Congress Catalog Card Number 76-1320
ISBN: 0-89221-020-6

CONTENTS

	Introduction	7
1	Wild	9
2	The Garden	17
3	Crop Rotation	24
4	Compost	26
5	Fruit Trees	27
6	Fruit Cellar	31
7	Cold Frames and Hotbeds	35
8	Canning	37
9	Drying	45
10	Corn Shelling	50
11	Bread	51
12	Hunting and Trapping	54
13	Salting and Smoking	57
14	Tanning	61
15	Horses	64
16	Goats	68
17	Butter and Cheese	74
18	Pigeons	77
19	Hogs	82
20	Rabbits	85
21	Chickens	89
22	Bees	94
23	The Pond	100
24	Fences	102
25	The Quonset Hut	106
26	The Barn	108
27	Midwifing	111
28	Sewing	116
29	Lighting	118
30	The Cabin	122
	Conclusion	131

INTRODUCTION

Woman in the Wilderness, "inspired" by Revelation 12:6, is to be used as a guide to survival in the end-times through faith in Jesus. The Lord is preparing places of refuge all over the world. Matthew 24:45 indicates that some of God's servants will be feeding His people food when He returns.

We are in the end-times. In this book, we will be sharing scriptures, experiences, food (spiritual and physical), recipes, animals, crops, buildings, facts and helps, a touch of humor, and a lot of faith.

We understand there is more to be said on almost every subject herein. We invite you to send us your ideas, recipes, experiences, walks, and prayers. Please share with us as we share with others.

Steve, Dee, Rick, Josheb, Mel, Merrybeth, Dirk, and Sundown send all our love, that you might find Him and eternal survival.

Behold, the eye of the Lord is upon them that fear him, upon them that hope in his mercy; To deliver their soul from death, and to keep them alive in famine. Our soul waiteth for the Lord: he is our help and our shield. For our heart shall rejoice in him, because we have trusted in his holy name. Let thy mercy, O Lord, be upon us, according as we hope in thee.

Psalm 33:18-22

A little over a year ago, my wife and I decided to celebrate our first anniversary at Holiday Inn and take a little time to figure out what the Lord wanted us to do. For two and a half weeks people had brought me seeds, plants, books, everything that had to do with farming, self-sufficiency, and how to grow things. I had decided when I was thirteen that farming definitely wasn't for me; it was too much work. The Lord seemed to have other plans, though.

I was satisfied with working in the coffeehouses and prisons, taking care of whomever came by, and riding my motorcycle. None of these had to do with farming.

When we arrived at the motel, my wife and I went to the pool to relax. I slid down in the whirlpool. The man sitting directly across from me, a short, rather heavy-set, red-faced gentleman from Canada, looked right at me and asked, "What do you do?"

I had made up my mind before I went there that I wasn't going to get involved in a witness or anything. I was just going to relax, think, and pray, not talk. So, I

answered rather reluctantly,
"I have a small farm."

The Lord put a big check on me, and said I'd better tell the man all of it. So I told him we were a Christ-centered coffeehouse and rehabilitation center.

He looked me right in the eye and said, "What you need are Jerusalem artichokes and sunflowers."

I didn't drown, needless to say, but I was shocked. One of the books I had received the previous week told how to grow sunflowers, and also mentioned that Jerusalem artichokes were an excellent crop. This was enough confirmation to continue.

Not long after the incident at the Holiday Inn, I was telling some of our friends from New Life Community near Grand Rapids, Michigan, about how the Lord was leading us. They provided us with the Jerusalem artichokes that they had growing wild along their fence rows.

The Jerusalem artichoke, not to be confused with the Globe artichoke, looks like a small sunflower above the ground and like a potato below the ground. They have a nut-like flavor. You can fry them, boil them, bake them, or use them in salads. They can also be used as a livestock food. Some advertisements listing artichokes say they will yield twenty tons of artichokes per acre. That's a lot of food!

I began to wonder what we had growing wild on our thirteen acres that could be used as food, that wouldn't have to be bought or farmed.

We started looking, digging around, and buying books to find out what we had. Most of the things come in four or five categories: Teas, greens, roots, nuts, berries. We are going to try to separate these for you.

Some time ago we were visiting a sister, Shirley Whipple, in Buffalo, New York. While dining at The Anchor, a restaurant known for its good food, we noticed the menu listed dandelion and burdock omelets. So, girls, it won't be as rough as you may think.

My trouble with herb teas is that most of them I've tried taste like grass to me. I was open to anything as long as it didn't taste like grass. I'll give you some of the things you can use for tea: strawberry leaves, rose hips (the little red berry on roses), red clover leaves, and raspberry leaves.

We have camomile. This is a plant with a very small white and yellow daisy that grows about eighteen to twenty-four inches high. The flowers are dried and used for tea. These flowers can also be boiled; remove the oil on top and use it as a hair rinse.

The sassafras tree is easily identified by the three different kinds of leaves. The young roots, cut into small pieces are used for tea.

Comfery is another, with a rather wide leaf. We harvest these leaves regularly, and they grow back. In some areas of the country, comfery is used as a hay. We would advise you raise this plant.

For those people who can't possibly do anything in the morning before they have a cup of coffee (I think even if the Lord came back they'd still want a cup of coffee first), we have good news. Dandelion roots can be dug up, washed, ground, and roasted to make a very good coffee substitute.

The Scriptures say: ". . . It is said, Thou shalt not tempt the Lord thy God" (Luke 4:12). I thought it was tempting the Lord a little extra to drink sumac, but surprisingly, the red berries make a nice red drink. When the berries are steeped and the liquid is served cool, it is similar to pink lemonade. This is something for the kids—the big kids, too.

We have mint growing wild by our mailbox. Mint can be used in making mint jelly, flavoring ice cream, meat, cold drinks, and peppermint drops.

Peppermint Drops
One cup honey, moistened with 2 T. water. Boil for 5 minutes, then take from fire and add cream of tartar the size of a pea, mix well. Add 4 or 5 drops of oil of peppermint and beat briskly until mixture whitens. Drop quickly onto oiled paper in drops about the size of peas. They can be easily removed by moistening paper on other side and scraping with a limber knife. Dry in a warm place on a sieve, and store in a closely covered box.

Pigweed is in abundant supply here. A neighbor who works in a bicycle shop gave my wife a handful of pigweed seed the other day. I looked at them a little strangely until I did some research. Pigweed seeds can be used as a grain cereal. They can be added to soups and breads, and when pigweed is young, the leaves can be cooked as greens.

I believe if I hadn't seen burdock on The Anchor's menu I might have skipped this one. The young leaves and shoots can be cooked as greens. The roots can be dried or roasted on the first-year plants. But stay away from old burdock! The leaves, like rhubarb leaves, are poisonous. Some of the burdock stalk can be used by simply peeling off the outside and eating the center of the stalk.

Lamb's quarters may be used like the pigweed, cooked as spinach, or the leaves can be eaten in a salad.

Plantain leaves may also be used in a salad or prepared as spinach.

The seeds and greens of red clover may also be eaten.

Now that it sounds like we're really cleaning up the yard, we'll tell you about quack grass. Quack grass grows wild to a height of about three feet in our hayfield. The grain on the top, resembling wheat, can be harvested and the roots can be eaten.

You can use the young stems of thistles by peeling and eating them.

I've been stung with so many nettles, I know you would never get me to eat any. But, the stalks and leaves can be cooked as greens. This will remove the stinging qualities.

Goldenrod seeds may be used in making mush; The leaves may be used for tea.

Horseradish was another of our experiences. Horseradish is best when dug in the spring before it develops broad leaves. The young plant's leaves are rather fern-like. After digging, cut the tops off as you would a carrot, and replant for next spring. Prepare the horseradish roots *outside*. Wash them and grind them through a food grinder. The fumes are very strong, so make sure there is cross-ventilation. Steve and Dee tried it inside once, even after a warning from Mel. Were they ever sorry! By the time they were finished, their eyes were bloodshot and they had cried a lot. After grinding the horseradish, salt it, and cover it with white vinegar. Put it in jars, and store in a refrigerator.

Wild garlic and onions have a hardier taste than the domestic varieties. These can be chopped into small pieces and dried to use as seasonings.

Since we have a lake, we have a good supply of cattails. The roots may be peeled, dried, and ground into a flour. The young shoots can be boiled just like asparagus. If you haven't got your Alpine down-filled sleeping bags, you can use mature cattail heads (in the fall) for filling blankets and making sleeping bags.

Some of the trees growing wild are black walnut and hickory. The nuts are very good in candy, cakes, cookies, ice cream, and breads. Other good nut trees are English walnut and chestnut. These must be planted in twos so they can cross-pollinate. To roast chestnuts, wash them, make a slit in the side of each one, and boil in enough water to cover them for ten minutes. Then drain, spread on a greased pan, and bake for ten minutes in a hot oven. Serve hot with salt.

We have hazelnut bushes, but we haven't harvested yet.

We have a Pawpaw tree. The fruit is tasty and has a flavor similar to bananas. I remember how much fun it was as a kid, to throw the over-ripe ones at each other. They really splotted!

Acorns, the fruit of the oak trees, are edible only after you leach the tannic acid from them. This is done by boiling the acorns, draining, washing, rinsing, and repeating the process two or three times until all acid is removed. Then you can make flour out of them or just eat them as a nut. Don't throw away the tannic acid for it can be used tanning hides, which we will talk about later. Refer to "Tanning," chapter 14.

Currants make a fine drink. In Sweden, currants are planted as shrubs around the house. The fruit is boiled and squeezed down to make a juice concentrate. Here are some recipes that you will want for currants, raspberries, or strawberries.

Currant Drops

Prepare the same as peppermint drops, except moisten honey with currant juice instead of water, set on the stove and melt, stirring constantly, but do not let it boil. Add a little more honey, warming it a moment with the rest. Drop on oiled paper.

Dried Currants

Put alternate layers of currants and sugar in a jar, use one cup of sugar to one pound of currants. Let it stand until the next day and boil it for 15 minutes. Skim, then dry in a slow oven or in the sun. Serves well in puddings or pies instead of raisins. Pack in sugar in glass jars.

We have wild strawberries, ground cherries, and black raspberries that we've used in jams, jellies, and other goodies. To dry raspberries, blanch them before laying them in the sun to dry.

Wild rice wasn't growing wild, so we planted it in the inlets of our lake. Wild rice has to be planted in running water so the water will be changed at least once a day. Rice makes the water stagnant, so the rice will die if it doesn't have this change of water. The best way to harvest rice is by canoe.

We have several large maple trees growing in our front lawn. We have discovered that the winged seeds may be roasted and eaten. Don't forget when the sap starts to run in the spring, you can collect it, boil it down, and make maple syrup.

Here's a good breakfast menu for you:
Golden Rod Mush
Maple Syrup
Cattail Toast w/ Strawberry Jam
Dandelion Coffee
Burdock Omelet (in season)

Jerusalem Artichoke

2-GARDEN

The righteous eateth to the satisfying of his soul, but the belly of the wicked shall want.
—Proverbs 14:25

Gardening is a lot of rewarding fun and work. Gardening is also a lot of trial and error in finding what works best for your soil and climate. Again and again someone will give you a new idea which several others will say is absolutely wrong.

Gardening ought to be a family project. Even children can learn to tend their own gardens when small plots are provided for them. If everyone pitches in, the work seems much smaller.

A garden can be small, or large. The only real requirements for a good garden are seeds or small plants, good soil, sunshine, water, and work.

It is a good idea to plan a garden in the fall. Choose a sunny location; Then and throughout the winter, apply manure to the soil for fertilizer. If the ground has never been turned over, do it in the fall to give the grass and weeds time to decay and produce a natural fertilizer.

If a garden has already been there, just plow or turn over the soil as soon as all produce is removed. As soon as possible in the spring, work the garden again with whatever equipment you have until all large dirt clods are broken up. In a large garden, a tractor, plow, and cultivator will be your best equipment. In smaller gardens, tillers are adequate. A hoe, shovel, push plow, and rake are necessities for any size garden. Of course, when you can't buy or sell without the mark of the beast, you won't be able to use tractors and tillers because you won't be able to buy gas. We will be cultivating our garden with our horse. The boys just bought an adjustable-row, one-horse cultivator, which we will be using.

Before getting new seeds, sit down and make a scale drawing of your garden. Plan the length of the rows and what will go in them. Most seed packages give directions on how to plant them and some seed catalogs will be helpful. But if this is your first garden, don't start out by planning a half pound of green beans for a small garden, unless you are sure you have room for them. (Beans yield at least three times per season.) We keep a record of gardening directions and our specific garden plan, improving it yearly.

The following chart is from our garden:

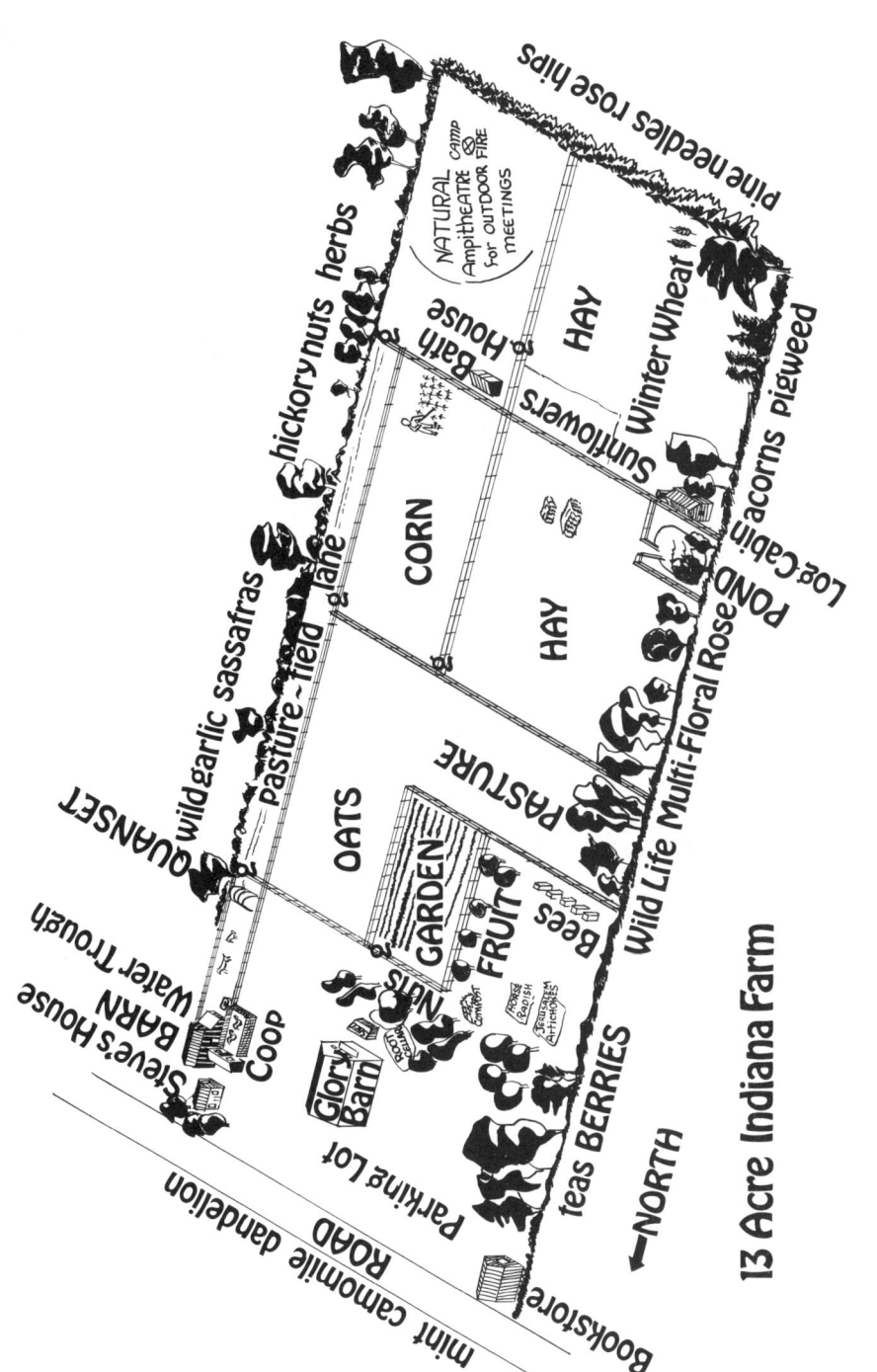

GARDEN CHART

	ROWS INCHES APART	SEEDS INCHES APART	SEEDS INCHES DEEP	PLANTS INCHES APART	TIPS
Asparagus	36		1½	18	SALT CAN BE USED TO CONTROL GRASS
Green Beans	18-30	2	1½		
Lima Beans	24-30	2-3	1½		
Beets	16-30	2-3	½		
Broccoli	30-36		¼	24-36	SIMILAR TO CAULIFLOWER
Brussel Sprouts	24-30	12-18	½		
Cabbage	24-30		½	12-20	
Carrot	15-30	2	½		SOW SEEDS 2" APART AND YOUR YIELD WILL BE HIGHER, BECAUSE YOU WON'T NEED TO THIN
Cauliflower	30		¼	24	
Celery	24-30	8	⅛		
Chives	10-16	8	½		HERB PLOT
Corn	30-36	12	2		*Plant Rows North &
Eggplant	24-30		¼	24	South so they get sun
Endive	18-30	12	¼		EVENLY.
Ground Cherry	30	24	½		
Kale	18-30	8-12	½		
Leeks	12-18	2-4	½		PLANT WITH HERBS IN ADJACENT PLOT
Muskmelon	4'-6'		1	4'-6'	
Onion Seeds	12-24	2-3	½		
Sets	12-24	2-3	1½		
Plants	12-24	2-3	2½		
Parsley	12-20	3-6	¼		PLANT IN HERB PLOT
Peppers	30	18-24	¼		
Potato	30	12	4		
Radish	6-30	1-2	½		USE WOOD-ASH FOR INSECTICIDE
Squash	12'		1½	12'	SOW ABOUT 6 SEEDS PER HILL
Tomato	30		½	36	PLANT ROWS ....
Turnip	15-30	1-3	½		

We decided to pray over, not spray our garden. This year our problem has been with deer getting in our garden, but that's the Lord supplying our meat. Hallelujah! These are the scriptures we stand on for insect repellent in our garden: "And shall no evil befall thee, neither shall any plague come nigh thy dwelling" (Ps. 91:10); "And whatsoever ye shall ask in my name, that will I do, that the Father may be glorified in the Son" (John 14:14). The Lord is faithful.

Last year, we didn't claim Psalm 91:10 for our garden, and He taught us a lesson. We put chlordane dust on the potatoes and green beans. It was too strong, and turned the plants yellow and stunted their growth. We still had potatoes and green beans, but the yield was not as good as it could have been.

Many people put herbs, asparagus, rhubarb, and grapes in small adjacent plots because these are perennial, coming up each year without replanting.

We planted our asparagus in a four-by-sixteen feet plot, in rows twelve inches apart. This vegetable is harvested in early spring, when the shoots are six to eight inches tall. Rhubarb is harvested regularly throughout the summer by cutting off the tender stalks. stalks.

Our grapes are planted five feet, six inches apart. We tied them loosely with binder twine on wires stretched three feet, six inches above the ground between fence posts. Four of the branches off the main trunk are trained to grow on these wires. Each fall, everything is pruned except the trunk and the four branches.

It is a lot more economical to start some seeds indoors six to eight weeks before planting, usually in late March or early April. It's not a good idea, however, to put them out before June 1, even when danger of frost is past, as they are more delicate than nursery plants.

When you've finally planned your garden and the soil is ready for the seeds, mark your rows. When using a tractor and cultivator, your rows are already marked by the cultivator. When you have only a hoe, you will need to mark your rows with stakes and strings. Do not remove the stakes and string until the plants are one to two inches high and up well throughout the row. This makes it easier to weed and distinguish between rows.

Most seeds can be planted directly in the garden after all danger of frost is past. Here is a chart that may help you plant your seeds and plants, along with some tips:

GARDEN LAYOUT

	6 ROWS CORN		
	4 ROWS GREEN BEANS		
	WAX BEANS		
	COWPEAS		
	MARIGOLDS & TOMATOES		
	LIMA BEANS		
	CARROTS		
	2 ROWS TOMATOES (ONE EARLY - ONE LATE)		
	KALE		
	RADISHES		
ENDIVE		BROCCOLI	
BEETS	CABBAGE		
CAULIFLOWER		EGGPLANT	
Squash & melons		Bell & CAYENNE PEPPERS, MARIGOLDS, TOMATOES	
		BROCCOLI	
		MARIGOLDS	
		TOMATOES	
		TOMATOES	
		TOMATOES	
		MARIGOLDS	
		TURNIPS, ENDIVE	
		MARIGOLDS, KALE	
		GRAPES	
ASPARAGUS	HERBS	ONIONS	
		Rhubarb	

← NORTH

When plants are six to eight inches tall, you can mulch around them with old straw, hay, or sawdust. This keeps the moisture in and weeds down. Last year we used sawdust, but put it on too early. It's the old parable of "I'll have the cleanest looking garden in town, and beat *you* to the swimming hole, too!"

Check your garden for weeds about once a week or more often if possible. These need to be pulled right away, as they will shade the plants and steal their food if left too long. After the weeds are pulled, they may be put back on the garden and allowed to decay for natural fertilizer and mulch.

After your plants are up, weeding is the only "work" needing to be done. "... if any would not work, neither should he eat" (2 Thess. 3:10).

After waiting so long for rain last year, Mel couldn't stand it any longer and bought a fifty dollar set of hose and sprinklers. Before he got it set up, it rained! The Lord promises us rain in due season. "Then I will give you rain in due season, and the land shall yield her increase, and the trees of the field shall yield their fruit" (Lev. 26:4).

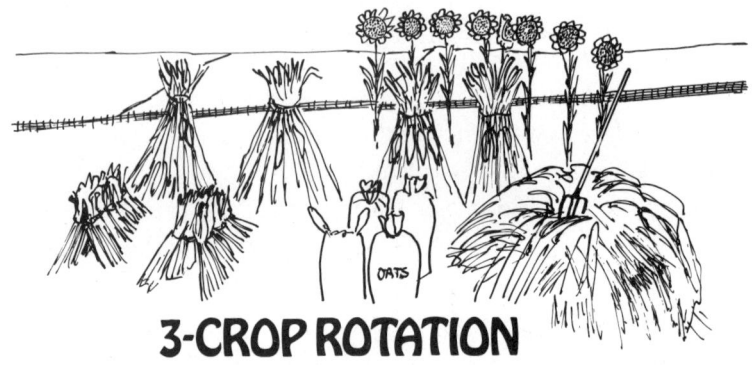

3-CROP ROTATION

Crop rotation builds up the soil, and you can get by without using a commercial fertilizer. Of course, you can supplement rotation with manure. Our crop rotation plan, given to us by a county agent, is a four-year rotation of corn, corn, oats, and pasture.

We're using Reed's Yellow Dent, an old-time, open-pollinated corn—it is a non-hybrid. This enables us to plant the fall's harvest in the spring for a new crop. It was recommended that we save the seed from the corn that, when matured, had nice, healthy stalks, and bent-over ears. This insures that the crop can stand in the field until harvest without fall rains getting into the end of the husk and rotting the corn. We also learned that the big round seeds in the center of the ear have to be used for next year's seeds.

We saw a method unusual to us, but not to farmers in 1912, to dry these ears of corn. Interweave the ears with binder twine and hang them up in the attic until they're dry.

The sunflowers we're growing will count the same as corn. So our rotation might run corn, sunflowers, oats, and the next year the field is to lay dormant in pasture. This is called a green manure crop. In the fall, the pasture will be turned over and planted in Hard Red Winter Wheat and Buckwheat.

The oats that we planted is the same kind the Amish use in this area of Indiana, Clinton 64. The heads and stalks mature at the same time which makes it easy for harvesting and putting into shocks. Our oats are planted with brome grass, Alsike, and white clover. The reason for this is, it will also be food for our bees. Alsike clover also has nodules that release nitrogen into the soil, thus acting as a natural fertilizer.

Any well-traveled area, such as our lane, can be made into another field. We've widened our lane from twenty feet to thirty-five feet and extended it the entire length of the farm. We intend to use this lane as pasture, planted with a grass called fescue. Fescue is used on ball diamonds, around school yards, and other heavy traffic areas because it won't die out from being trampled.

We're going to be able to utilize almost every square inch of our thirteen acres for something.

4-COMPOST

Compost pile is another very good way to obtain fertilizer for the garden. To construct a compost pile, put up a wire fence or snow fence to surround the compost and let air into the compost. "Compost," to most people, means scraps from the kitchen. Most of our garbage from our kitchen goes to our own garbage disposal here, the hogs. But you can make a compost pile out of bones, leaves, wood ashes to provide potash, feathers and innards from the chickens you've killed, small dead animals, sawdust, any grain that might have spoiled, any of the things from the garden, old wet hay, weeds, anything that will decay. Water your compost and stir it occassionally to aid the decomposing.

In three months the compost is ready to apply to your garden. Just scoop it up and apply as a fertilizer.

We've considered sludge, but haven't tried it yet. Chicago has been making sludge for years—dehydrating the sewage and taking out the harmful things, such as chemicals and soaps, that might kill plants. This sludge can be had in our area free for the hauling. We feel it would be an excellent source of fertilizer.

5-FRUIT TREES

"And God said 'Behold, I have given you . . . every tree, in which is the fruit of a tree yielding seed; to you it shall be for meat' " —(Gen. 1:29).

You must first decide what kind of tree is best for you. There are dwarf, semi-dwarf, and regular trees available. All of these take different periods of time to bear fruit. We decided the best tree for us would be a semi-dwarf, since they bear within two to three years. Although the semi-dwarf category is not large, it was still exciting to look at seed catalogs, see all the pictures of the apples, and pick out the kind that was best for us.

We settled on a self-pollinating Golden Delicious apple tree which bears early and plentifully. This apple is good for eating, cooking, and storing. They can be stored in the fruit cellar and kept all winter.

We chose the Alberta peach tree; the peaches are good canners and very delicious. We are not experimenting with the different varieties. We are sticking with the old varieties, the tried and true kinds. We will be drying many of our peaches. To do this, rub the peaches well with a piece of flannel to remove fuzz, and dry them in the sun.

Peach Chips

Use one cup of sugar to each pound of fruit. Boil sugar in enough water to dissolve it, and continue boiling until mixture becomes a thick syrup. Add peeled and sliced peaches, and scald them. Remove the peaches with a skimmer and dry them in the sun. When dry, pack the peaches closely in layers in jars.

A bing cherry tree was a must for our orchard. We also planted Schmidt's Biggareau Cherry tree near it so we would have cross-pollination. Schmidt's Biggareau will be used just for canning, and the bing will be for table use. I doubt whether we'll ever see any dried or canned bings. But, to dry the cherries, pit, stem, and dry them in the sun. If juice runs from them, spread it back on them and cover them with it.

We have Bartlett pears, which are good as dessert and in cooking, too.

Our apricots are Early Orange; these will be dried, canned, and perhaps made into jams.

You can see by now that we enjoy having a wide variety of foods. For example, we have apples, peaches, cherries, pears, and apricots in our orchard. It is important to have variety so you don't get bored. You could eventually get bored of steak and baked potatoes with sour cream, I'm sure. In everything we do, we want a large variety to choose from. This gives us more to pass on to you, so whatever your needs happen to be, we'll have a large enough variety throughout the farm to help you.

Some of our best sources of information are books brought by friends and acquaintances. Several weeks ago, brother Jerry Burkitt brought us some old school books, copyrighted in 1912, 1932, and 1933, about agriculture. One of the books, *Farm Projects and Farm Problems for Elementary Schools*, has really been a blessing. We would advise you to see if you can find some of these in your library.

We've also been blessed with finding old cookbooks at flea markets which tell about different techniques of canning, how to dry fruit, and how to store fruit in your fruit cellar. A few days ago, I bought an old *White House Cookbook*, and it is a store of information. So, get into your attics and your local flea markets and get some help!

The procedure we follow closely regarding planting, maintenance, and pruning of trees is found in James 1:5: "If any of you lack wisdom, let him ask of God, that giveth to all men liberally, and upbraideth not; and it shall be given him."

Instead of spraying our trees, we believe and confess Psalm 91:10: "There shall no evil befall thee, neither shall any plague come nigh thy dwelling."

To prevent insect attacks and plagues, we practice John 14:14: "And whatsoever ye shall ask in my name, that will I do, that the Father may be glorified in the Son."

There is no reason why you should have any trouble with these so-called problems!

When pruning our trees, we do it in the confidence that God said He would bless the work of our hand:

"The Lord shall open unto thee His good treasure, the heaven to give the rain unto thy land in His season and to bless all the work of thine hand . . ." (Deut. 28:12).

Basically, trees are pruned to remove undesireable parts, such as dead branches. This thinning process allows light to reach all parts of the tree, and produces higher quality fruit. There should be only a small amount of pruning on a tree.

NOTE: I want to tell you what happened as I prepared this chapter. I was in the cabin recording the material on tape so Dee could transcribe it. I had just finished recording all the promises in the scripture which are listed in this chapter. I stopped to make myself a cup of coffee and played the tape back to see if I had missed anything. The devil left everything on but the scriptures. This is the second time this has happened to me. We just have to rebuke the devil so he takes his hands off and the Lord is glorified in this whole book.

6-FRUIT CELLAR

First of all, decide if you really do need a fruit cellar. We wanted a fruit cellar to store our large quantity vegetables such as potatoes and turnips.

All the older farms in our area have fruit cellars. We did some investigating and found that the major complaint about fruit cellars was that they were too moist. These were laid up with rocks with no water proofing on the outside. But, if your fruit cellar is constructed right, there should be enough moisture coming up through the floor. The floor should not be stone or concrete; we're making our floor out of sand. Another must is proper ventilation. At one end of our fruit cellar, near the floor, will be a ventilation pipe going through to the roof. At the other end, near the door, will be a vent in the ceiling. So, there will be ventilation moving through the cellar at all times.

Now the problem was the location. Where would we put our fruit cellar? We picked a spot between our barn and our garden near the orchard which we thought had proper drainage. It's one of the highest spots on the farm, and when we had dug about one foot, we hit clay.

It's hard, old Indiana blue clay. So, the digging of the hole is going very slowly.

Out one end of the fruit cellar, we had to dig a drainage ditch. You should give a little more consideration to the direction your drainage ditch than we did. Two or three years before, a sewage drainage field had been put in. So, halfway into digging our ditch, you guessed it, we hit it. We had to go below the field. So there are a lot of things to consider; one can't just say, "Here, dig!"

You might want to put your fruit cellar against an existing cellar wall. Make a hole in the side wall of the cellar, so that you may go into your fruit cellar from your cellar. You might want to set it against your barn bank, if you have one.

The wall of our fruit cellar will be laid up with cement block. The roof will be made out of pieces left over from our quonset hut. We're going to shore up these pieces of corrugated metal so they won't come down while we pour approximately six inches of concrete and rocks on top for the ceiling. The fruit cellar will be approximately four to five feet into the ground, and will make a small mound on top of the ground. We will cover the whole thing with dirt and then sod it.

The entrance will be like the old cellar entrances you've seen on the outside of old houses; inside will be another insulated door. In the sand floor, you may transplant your endive, celery, leeks, lettuce, and other greens before frost. Water them occasionally, and you will have greens almost all winter long. You will also want to store in your fruit cellar tomatoes that haven't quite ripened before frost. These will last until Thanksgiving or later. Vegetables such as turnips, carrots, and beets may be put in boxes in the fruit cellar and covered with sand to prevent them from shriveling up and spoiling. We will also be growing mushrooms in the sand.

You won't have to be worried about bringing the artichokes in and covering them up. Artichokes, like horseradish and parsnips, may be left in the ground all winter and dug when you want them.

Because pumpkins and squash require cool dry air, we've been keeping them in a unheated, second-floor room of the Barn. Do not store these in the fruit cellar. We've put our squash, with alternating layers of straw, in a large box. These can be kept into late February and March.

Another type of storage is a wooden barrel, sunken in a hole. Dig a hole that is one-half the depth of the barrel, and two feet wider than the diameter of the barrel. Place the barrel in the center of the hole and fill in the hole around the barrel one foot deep with small pebbles and stones for a drain. The top part is rounded out with a layer of dirt, a layer of straw or hay, another layer of dirt, and then a board with a rock for a weight. Apples, potatoes, pears, and other foods can be stored in this barrel. Although this is a much cheaper and quicker way, we want to have our fruit cellar because we will be using it a lot.

Another storage idea that we intend to try is an icehouse. The icehouse that we will build will be a relatively small shed-type construction, possibly eight by twelve feet. We'll have small cracks in the floor for drainage, and heavily insulated walls and roof. We'll be cutting ice out of our lake and pond and storing it in the ice house. We've spotted some tongs that the old-timers used to use to haul ice out of the lake with horses. So, eventually we hope to get some tongs, put Stormy in harness, and use him to pull the ice to our shed. Dee's dad, Ray, says that once we get our ice into the shed, every layer and every block of ice has to be covered with sawdust so the blocks don't freeze together.

    As we've mentioned before, if you have a better idea or a more workable plan, we invite you to write us and share with us your idea.

7-COLD FRAMES & HOT BEDS

The cold frame is the same as the solar dryer illustrated in Chapter 9, but it has no vents to let the air pass through. Add heat to the cold frame and it will immediately become a hotbed. The reason you will eventually want to get into using cold frames and hotbeds is to insure seedlings for your garden. When we are unable to buy and sell, we won't be going to our local nursery and getting so many onion plants, tomato plants, or cabbage plants; we'll be raising seedlings in flats. We'll take these from inside the house, set them in cold frames, and try to keep the temperature between 60° and 70°. On hot days the lids will have to be ajar to ventilate the seedlings so they won't just steam and cook right there. At night, the lid should be closed. As long as the temperature doesn't drop below 40°, they will be reasonably safe.

Cold frames and hotbeds can be eliminated if you have a greenhouse where you arrange everything in flats. You might want to investigate some of the small commercial greenhouses that are now being built; we haven't decided to do that yet. One of the nice things we've seen is a small unit that is built right into a window. You just open or take out your window, set the unit in, and use it for a small garden of plants. Another way would be to build a larger unit that fits into the south side of the house where all the sunlight's available.

By the way, coldframes should face the south, the same as the greenhouses do. We've seen greenhouses that are domes, redwood design, and all sizes and shapes. We advise you to check these out.

8-CANNING

Canning turned out to be a real experience for me. I had never canned or even seen it done in my life, but I was enthusiastic about trying it. People often try to make it seem harder than it really is. It's one of the easiest things you can do on the farm. The rewards of canning can't be seen until the end of the season. Often you might think canning is a never-ending job because your vegetables keep producing.

We can all the produce from our garden, and by the end of the season, it's a real blessing to see all the different colors of food on the shelves.

There are two main methods of canning: water bath and pressure. In water bath canning, the jars are covered with boiling water and processed for a long period of time. In pressure canning, there are only about two quarts of water in the canner, but the process is considerably shorter than the water bath method. When using the water bath, start the water boiling while you are preparing the produce to be canned. Processing time starts when the jars are in the canner and the water is boiling. When pressure canning, processing time is started when the proper pressure has been reached. Adjust the heat for an even pressure level. After time is completed, remove canner from heat and wait for pressure to go completely to 0. Then remove weight gauge and open canner, lifting the back side of the lid first to prevent the steam from burning you.

Another kind of water bath canning is the outside canner that we have used. Some friends of ours from Tennessee helped us construct this canner. We dug a pit and lined it with cement blocks. We rested two iron poles on the cement blocks, making sure they were level, and set the washtub on these poles over the fire in the pit. We covered the tub with a tin lid to keep the heat in, and put wooden slats in the bottom of the washtub so the jars wouldn't get too hot and burst. After the canning was done, we slipped a fence post through the handles of the washtub to remove it from the fire. We canned twenty-three quarts at once this way. This old Kentucky-Tennessee method is cheap and time-saving. If we would have done these in a regular water bath canner, it would have taken a longer time.

There are also two methods of packing your fruits, vegetables, and meats: hot-pack and cold-pack. Hot-pack is partially cooking the food to be canned, then packing it in the jars, covering with the food's own liquid, and processing. Cold-pack is packing the jars with uncooked food, covering with boiling liquid, then processing.

There are some essentials to follow in canning. First, pick your fruits or vegetables early in the morning, while the dew is still on. This is when your produce is the freshest and crispiest. Another "rule of thumb" in canning is that it should be no longer than two hours between picking and canning.

To prepare vegetables for canning, wash thoroughly. Make sure the jars do not have any nicks or cracks. If they do, they will not seal. Throw them away or find another use for them. Tightly pack vegetables in clean, hot jars, leaving one-half to one inch headspace. Add one teaspoon salt, pour boiling water in the jars, leaving headspace. Wipe off rim, put lids on, and process. A chart is provided for you for both water bath and pressure canning times. Do not remove sealing bands until twelve hours after processing. When sealed, the dome lid will be concave. Store the canned goods in a dark, dry place under 70°. Darkness keeps the food from bleaching out. Date the jars and add any specific directions.

CANNING CHART

FRUIT	PRESSURE 5 lb. PINT	5 lb. QUART	WATER BATH PINT	QUART
Apples	8 min.	8 min.	15 min.	20 min.
Apricots	8 "	8 "	25 "	30 "
Berries	8 "	8 "	10 "	15 "
Cherries	8 "	8 "	20 "	25 "
Grapes	8 "	8 "	20 "	25 "
Peaches	8 "	8 "	25 "	30 "
Pears	8 "	8 "	25 "	30 "
Plums	8 "	8 "	20 "	25 "
Rhubarb	5 "	5 "	10 "	10 "

CANNING CHART

VEGETABLE	PRESSURE 10 lbs. PINT	10 lbs. QUART	WATER BATH PINT	QUART
Asparagus	25 min.	30 min.	3 hrs.	
Green Beans	20 "	25 "	3 hrs.	
Lima Beans	20 "	25 "	3 hrs.	
Wax Beans	40 "	50 "	3 "	
Beets	30 "	35 "	2 "	
Broccoli	30 "	35 "	2½ "	
Cabbage	30 "	35 "	2 "	
Carrots	25 "	30 "	2 "	
Cauliflower	30 "	35 "	2½ "	
Corn	55 "	85 "	3½ "	
Cowpeas	35 "	40 "	3 "	
Eggplant	30 "	40 "		
Endive	70 "	90 "	3 "	
Kale	45 "	70 "	3 "	
Squash or Pumpkin	55 "	90 "	3 "	
Tomatoes (5 lb.)	10 "	10 "	35 min.	45 min.
Potatoes New	30 "	40 "	3 hrs.	
Sweet	65 "	95 "	3 "	

MEAT CANNING CHART

	PREPARATION:	PRESSURE CANNER	PINT	QUART
BEEF VEAL LAMB PORK VENISON	Clean with damp cloth. Soak venison in salt water 1 to 2 hrs. (¼ cup salt to 1 qt. water). Drain. Cut in cubes or jar-length strips (grain runs length of jar). Remove bones, gristle, and fat. **COLD PACK:** Pack raw meat loosely to 1" of top of jar. Add no liquid. Put open jars in deep pan with warm water 2" below rim of jars; Cover pan. Simmer about 75 min. or medium done or 170° in center of jars. Add salt, put on lids. Process in pressure canner.		75 min.	90 min.
	HOT PACK: Cook meat, covered in small amount of water until medium done; stir occasionally. Pack jars loosely to 1" of top of jar. Add salt. Cover with broth or boiling water leaving 1" from top. Put on lids. Process in pressure canner.		75 min.	90 min.
POULTRY: CHICKEN DUCK TURKEY GAME BIRDS RABBIT	Wash poultry in cold water. Soak rabbit in salt water (¼ cup salt to 1 qt. water) 1 to 2 hrs. Wipe-cut up. **COLD PACK:** Debone but leave skin. Pack loosely in jars. (Poultry - place breasts in center legs with skin next to glass.) Leave 1" head space. Put open jars in large pan with warm water 2" below top of jars. Cover pan till center of jars is 170° or medium done - about 75 min. Add salt, if desired, put on lids. Process in Pressure Canner.		75 min.	90 min.
	HOT PACK: Cook poultry covered in small amount of hot broth or water till almost no pink shows in cut center. Debone. Pack loosely in jars. (Pack poultry same as above). Leave 1" head space, add salt if desired. Cover with boiling broth leaving 1" headspace. Put on lids, process in pressure Canner.		75 min.	90 min.

To prepare fruits for canning, prepare the same as vegetables, omitting salt, and pouring boiling syrup in the jars instead of water. The syrup consistency is up to the individual. For a *very* light syrup: 1 cup sugar to 4 cups water. For light syrup, 2 cups sugar to 4 cups water. Medium syrup: 3 cups sugar to 4 cups water. Heavy syrup: 4 3/4 cups sugar to 4 cups water. The syrup should be boiled 5 minutes before pouring on fruit. If you are using honey instead of sugar, use 1/2 cup honey for every cup of sugar called for.

An easy way to make applesauce is to quarter the apples after washing them and put them in a pan with just enough water to keep them from burning. Boil the apples until soft. Put in a foodmill or colander, and mash the pulp through. The seeds and peelings will not go through. All you do now is add sugar to taste, and maybe a little cinnamon. This can be frozen or canned. To can them, put the jars in a pressure canner, five lbs. pressure for five minutes, or water bath canner for fifteen minutes.

In canning plums and cherries, the skins should be pricked with a straight pin or needle to keep them from bursting in the jars.

When hot-packing fruits, boil the fruit in the desired syrup for five munutes and then process in the same liquid.

There is a chart provided as a guide for how much food to can for a family of six.

ITEMS & QUARTS NEEDED FOR FAMILY OF SIX

Broccoli	24 qts.
Carrots	20 qts.
Squash	20 qts.
Tomatoes	60 qts.
Juice	120 qts.
Peppers	22 qts.
Cauliflower	36 qts.
Green Beans	60 qts.
Peas	24 qts.
Sweet Corn	36 qts.
Lima Beans	24 qts.
Beets	12 qts.
Pumpkin	12 qts.

Here are some recipes you might like to try:

Piccalilli:
        5 green tomatoes
        5 green peppers
        2 red bell peppers
        5 peeled onions
        1 small cabbage

Chop on coarse blade in food grinder. Cover with 1/4 cup salt. Do not prepare in metal! Let stand overnight. Cover with cold water, drain.

Add: 3 cups brown sugar
        1 1/2 t. celery seed
        1 T. mustard seed
        1 T. whole cloves
        2" stick cinnamon

1 T. allspice berries
2 cups mild vinegar

Add to tomato mixture, bring to boiling and boil for 15 minutes. This will make four pints. No processing in canner! Put in hot jars, and put on the lids; it will seal on its own.

Pickled Peppers:
4 qt. banana peppers
1 1/2 cups salt
2 cloves of garlic
2 T. horseradish
10 cups vinegar
2 cups water
1 1/4 cups sugar

Cut two small slits in each pepper. Dissolve salt in 4 cups water. Pour over peppers, and let stand overnight. Cover with cold water, drain. Rinse and drain. Combine remaining ingredients, simmer 15 minutes. Remove garlic and pack in jars leaving 1/4" headspace. Pour remaining pickling liquid over peppers. Hot water bath for 10 minutes for pints, 15 minutes for quarts.

9-DRYING

This whole book is designed for the Christian to be able to escape the mark of the beast, 666, that is talked about in Revelation. We believe there will come a time when canning will not be available to us because we cannot buy the lids. Some of you ladies know how scarce these lids are right now. I'm sure if it comes down to deciding whether the Christians or other people are going to get lids, the Christians just won't get them. This is why we recommend that you explore drying. It is a fun experience that gives a sense of accomplishment.

Our first experience with drying was making jerky from venison. We soaked it all night in salt water, sprinkled it with pepper, and hung it in an oven we have that sits on top of our stove. Ours is one of the old ovens that would work on one of the Old Perfection kerosene ranges. These ovens are made for campers, and can be found at sporting goods stores.

We sliced our jerky in long strips 1/4 -inch thick, hung it on racks in our oven, and set the heat as low as possible, approximately 120°. We have made the mistake of putting the heat too high, so that the meat cooks and becomes hard and undesirable to chew. It must be a very slow drying process; leave the oven door ajar several inches at the top so that the moisture will be able to escape.

There are several things from which you can make jerky. You can, of course, dry beef. The Indians used small animals, such as squirrel. They would take the squirrel, clean it, and pulverize it, bones and all. They would make the whole thing 1/4-inch thick, dry it, and eat it like that. I haven't tried that personally yet, but I'd like to. You can get your own recipes and be creative. The old-time jerky and hardtack can really fill you up.

Hardtack

To 4 cups of flour, add 2 T. salt and 2 T. sugar. Gradually add water to make a stiff dough. Pat it down to 1/4" thick, cut it into strips, place on a greased cookie sheet, and place in approximately 300° oven until dry, but not brown.

You can dry fish in the same way you dry beef or venison. We have a very small pan fish which we will dry or smoke. Cut the heads off and then split the body. Don't cut clear through the tail, though, so you can hang the fish over a rack. When the fish is nearly cut in two, take out the guts, salt the inside a little bit, and hang the fish so you have one half of it on one side of the rack, and one half on the other side.

Another type of drying is solar drying, using just the sun. An outdoor dryer can be built a lot like a cold frame with a glass top from an old storm window. You want to have slits around the top and bottom covered with screen so that the air can circulate and insects can't get in. You can rotate your food every few hours. Some of the apples and pears may take several days to dry, but it is well worth the effort. We dried apples last year and the kids got into them just like candy. We sprinkled them with a little sugar or a little cinnamon. Needless to say, it's a lot better than candy for your children. After these fruits are dried, you can restore them to near their original condition by adding hot water and letting them set for a little while.

We have also dried corn. Cut the kernels off the cob and dry them like you would anything else from the garden. If you want to bring it back to life, soak it overnight in sweet milk. We've dried sweet corn on the cob as a whole corn, then parched it. This is good and filling. Put a very little bit of grease in an iron skillet. Turn the heat on medium high. Keep a lid on the corn since it pops. You can shake the pan. When it's done exploding, you can put a little more grease in and sprinkle it with salt. It's really good.

We've also dried celery and lima beans. We're going to be making our own dried vegetable soup.

One of the methods we tried for preserving green beans was taken out of the *Foxfire* book. It said that the Appalachian people left these beans whole, snipping off only the ends. Then they hung them on a string and put them in the attic where it was warm to let them dry. The nickname of these was "leatherbritches." While we were picking these beans and stringing them and hanging them in the attic, the question kept going through our heads: Why do they call these leatherbritches? After they were dried, we let them soak all night in a little soda or salt water, and cooked them like regular beans. When we ate some of them, the name was no longer a mystery. They are really tough! The flavor is good, but they are very chewy. We're doing some of our beans this way. It's a good way to keep them.

A neighbor, a native of Kentucky, told us that what he remembered most about drying was dried pumpkin rings. They cut pumpkins in 1 to 1 1/2-inch rings, put them on a broomstick, hung it beside the fireplace between two chairs and dried them. He said that when they would go coon hunting or trapping they'd always grab a couple pieces of pumpkin. It's very pleasant to chew on.

We have also dried mint and catnip. This year we planted our whole herb garden with chives, lavender, leeks, lemon balm, parsley, rosemary, sage, and thyme. In drying the herbs, place them in a paper bag, tie a string around the bag, and hang it in your attic. When they dry, the leaves fall off in the bag. This is a convenient way to store them.

When drying berries, most of them, like raspberries, should be blanched for about thirty seconds before drying. An old cookbook that we found at the flea market has a recipe for making a dried fruitcake. Put a bunch of peaches or apricots together, mash them down to make a solid cake out of them, and shape approximately 3 or 4 inches across and 2 inches deep. Dry the cake in your oven or solar. This is what they used to do on long sea voyages and journeys so they could always have fresh fruit.

My experience with fruit leather was rather disheartening at first. I didn't cook it long enough or something. Pit and peel the fruit you want to make leather out of and boil the fruit pulp until mushy. Pour the mixture on a cookie sheet and let it dry. When it's dry, it can be cut into strips or rolled up. You can also make little candies out of them for individual servings. At the time of this book, I haven't made a very successful fruit leather. If you readers come up with a good recipe, we would be interested in it.

10-SHELLER

We intend to shell our corn, then dry it and grind it. We've obtained an old-time, hand-operated corn sheller. It has a motor on it now, but when we cannot buy electricity without taking the mark of the beast, we will discard the motor and hand-operate it.

When the corn is removed and dried, we will be putting it through a hand-operated grinder. To make cornmeal, we will use the same procedure that we use for our wheat meal in making flour. One of the ladies from Tennessee that stopped by recently suggested that we use lye to remove the yellow hull of the corn to make hominy. Let the hominy dry, and then grind it to make a white cornmeal.

The empty corn-cobs may be used in the old cookstove, as the old-timers used to do.

Your natural food stores of hardwares would have hand-operated grain mills now. We found ours, again, with the Amish.

11-BREAD

"But He answered and said, It is written, Man shall not live by bread alone . . ." —Matt. 4:4

Every batch of dough I touched turned into mandatory bread. We had to eat it—like it or not!

Steve and I moved into the Glory Barn on December 10, 1973, with me seven months pregnant, Steve burnt out on dope, and both of us needing the Lord. Steve went to work on the Barn, and I in the kitchen. My first experience in the Glory Barn kitchen was baking bread, but my loaves of bread turned out like bricks for about six weeks.

Mel kept asking me, "Is this what you call bread? Wow!"

You see, this bread I made weighed in at close to three pounds a loaf, measured nine inches long and two inches high, had a very hard crust, and was doughy inside. Neither the dogs nor the chickens would eat it. Exodus 23:25 says: ". . . and He shall bless thy bread and thy water . . ." He really had to, because even after blessing it, it was pretty bad.

Finally, after six weeks of mandatory bread, Mel's Aunt Nora came by. Aunt Nora knows just about everything about everything.

I thought six weeks of mandatory bread was due season enough (see Prov. 15:23), so I asked her why my bread wasn't rising right. Mel kept saying, "Knead it longer!" This didn't help, either. Then Aunt Nora told me the water temperature wasn't right. I was ruining the yeast by using water either too hot or too cold.

Mel had given me an any-fool-can-make-it recipe; I couldn't make it, so I cried myself to sleep, and wasn't too enthused about making "bricks" again. After Aunt Nora's advice, however, I tried again, and was successful.

Bread

    1 1/2 c. lukewarm water

        The water temperature is right when you stick your finger in the water and feel neither hot nor cold, just wet.

    1 T. or 1 pkg. yeast (dry active or cake)

    1 T. sugar

    1 1/2 t. salt

    2 T. melted shortening or oil

    6 c. flour

    Dissolve yeast in water, add sugar, salt and shortening or oil. Gradually stir flour in well. Cover with damp cloth and let rise in a warm, draft-free place for one hour. Knead on a lightly floured board or table. (Kneading is working the dough with the heels of your hands and pushing away from you. Then, fold the top half of the dough over the bottom half, turn dough to the left or right about 1/4 of the way around and push again.) Knead the dough for about 10 minutes. Cover and let rise again for one hour. Knead as before. Shape dough into a loaf and place into a greased loaf pan. Cover and let rise for 1/2 hour. Bake at 450° for 15 minutes. Lower heat to 425° and bake for 25 minutes. This makes one loaf.

We will be planting Hard Red Winter Wheat and grinding our own flour for bread. One cup wheat makes 1 1/2 cups of flour. This homeground flour is not as absorbent as commercially prepared flour, so you will need more of this flour than the prepared. Gauge the amount by feeling the kneading consistency. If the dough is sticky, add more flour.

We have also found a good yeast recipe. It is called milk yeast or salt-rising.

1 pint new milk
1 t. salt
2 T. flour

Add salt to milk, beat in flour for 1/2 minute. Pour into pitcher and place pitcher in a kettle of warm water. Keep it warm, but not hot. Let rise for five hours. Water can be substituted for the milk.

To make the bread, mix rising with one quart warm water and a pinch of salt. Stir flour in until consistency is that of a stiff sponge and let rise again for one hour. Mold and put in pans to bake at 425° for 30 to 35 minutes.

Deuteronomy 28:12—"The Lord shall open unto thee His good treasure, . . . and to bless the work of thine hand: . . ."

12-HUNTING & TRAPPING

This chapter is a little humiliating to me because I missed two deer this year. The skills we're going to talk about here—shooting and trapping—have to be practiced. I don't know if you'll ever get over buck fever. I think I'm going to pray for and claim by faith an early manifestation for my buck fever.

First, we'll talk about weapons. I have a .22 rifle and a small .410 gauge shotgun. We're not hoarding shells or trying to rely on guns as supplying our wild game. As I said, I missed two deer this year, so praise the Lord! The Lord is going to have to bring me the animals. The guns will be no good to you if you have to buy shells. And shells are only good for so long a time, and then they won't fire.

I'm a pretty good shot with a bow, but I'd hate to rely on my skill in archery for food. That's not to say that you can't.

Most people think that a good knife is a big knife. I've seen a lot of guys walking through the woods with Bowie-type knives. These knives may be good for chopping down a tree, but they are of little value in scaling fish or skinning animals.

I think any knife with a four-inch blade is sufficient. It's worth the money to invest in a good knife; you're not going to get a good knife for $10 at a truck stop. I also have a leather strap on my knife sheath, so if I have to work around water, I can slip this leather strap around my wrist, and not be concerned about losing my knife. I'd say a knife is one of the most important things to have.

I feel trapping is a better way of obtaining food. The fishtraps we make are a cylinder-type with one cone. You can also make them with two cones. We used one cone in the end with a small built-in trap door to let the fish out. We make trap out of one-inch by two-inch wire. This is like a hardware cloth that you would use for fencing. Due to the fact that your holes are that size, you never get any small fish. This is to let the small fish continue to grow. I might add that as far as I know, these are legal only in private lakes and small ponds.

Our best luck at setting the trap was in four to six feet of water along the shoreline, preferably at an inlet or outlet. I suggest that you use a wire or a rope to secure the trap to the bank. This makes it easier to find and prevents losing the trap.

A trout line is also good. You set it at night, and run it two or three times a night to catch catfish. One brother in the Body has built a turtle trap, which is similar to the fishtrap.

Animal traps come in two different kinds: snares and deadfalls. Almost any Boy Scout book would illustrate these basic designs.

I believe we should pray about everything we do. This

includes fishing and hunting as well as the care of crops, trees, and animals. The Lord is going to have to guide us in the end-times and He would like to have us trust Him in all ways. I don't think there's anything too small to bother God with, such as where to place your traps. I read about some men who had trouble fishing. But, after the Lord told them to put their net on the other side of the boat, they caught more fish than they could haul in, and broke the net, too. I'm not trying to make light of this. I'd encourage you to pray about your hunting and fishing.

13-SALTING & SMOKING

There is a fine line between hoarding and faith. People who criticize hoarding say that you don't have enough faith in Christ to make it through any end-time trials. We're not hoarding; it's just not scriptural. We're not going to lose our faith in Christ; we've prayed about everything we've done, including buying salt. The Lord told us we could get some salt. I had only a vague idea of how we could use salt. While we were still praying about what to do with it, I ordered 1,000 pounds of utility salt from the local grocery. Before ordering the salt, I never had any trouble with the people at the grocery. They really made fun of me for buying so much salt, though. I felt the anointing and knew it was on me. I had bought some grape juice for communion, too, and they were kidding me about that. I really felt it was of the Lord. I just shrugged it off, paid for the salt and communion juice, and came on home with ten or twelve bags of salt.

A few days after I got the salt, Kathy, one of the girls who has been with us since the Barn started, brought me the *Old Virginia Cookbook* which explained how you could keep meat fresh by salting. You know, I'm like most of you, I've had the presence of the Lord going with me. This was a good confirmation when Kathy gave me a cookbook on how to use the salt.

I shared the idea of *Woman in the Wilderness* with about twenty brothers and sisters in New Life Community in Michigan. I told them what we were doing here and what the Lord was leading us into, purposely leaving out salt. When I finished, I asked them if the Lord had impressed them to begin keeping anything. One brother looked right at me, and said the Lord had told him to keep salt. I hope you don't have a problem with this, but I've prayed about it, I got an answer, and it's been confirmed twice.

There was also Bob, a guy from New York, who brought six or seven 100-pound bags of salt to me that he said the Lord had told him to bring. By this time, I was being well blessed by confirmations. I asked him if the Lord told him to bring it, what was I supposed to use it for? I thought I already had enough salt for my purposes. He said the Lord told him we were going to use it for an exchange like money. Salt is one thing we can't extract around here.

I read there are ways to salt vegetables and keep them for a long period of time. We still feel that our vegetables are better by drying them.

The experiences I've had with curing bacon and hams have come from our neighbor, Possum. Possum said that the ratio of salt would be one peck of salt to approximately 500 pounds of pork. This recipe pertains to all parts of the hog: mid-section, ham, shoulders, and bacon.

Salting pork

Put salt in five gallons of water to make brine. Then, take four pounds of salt, two pounds of brown sugar, and depending on taste, one or two teaspoons of cayenne pepper. (Don't use metal!) Rub bacon thoroughly in the salt and brown sugar mixture, pack it tightly in a crock, and cover with brine. Leave in brine for four to seven weeks. Then smoke it. The smoking that was done here was done in a small icebox and was complete in two days. (See sketch for instructions on making an old refrigerator into a smokehouse in Chapter 30.

Smoking is done over a "cold smoke." A small hickory fire, a fire of corn-on-cobs, preferably sweet corn, can be used. Don't make a large fire; just a smoke. Put your ham in a brown paper bag and hang it socket side down so it will drain. Be sure the bag is tightly tied so it will keep the insects out.

When you get ready to use the bacon or ham, don't be afraid if there is mold on the outside. Take a sharp knife and peel off the mold.

We have another recipe for curing ham, called "the Old Virginia" way. Salt the hams down for five or six weeks. Then brush the hams off and rub them with hickory ashes. Let them lay in these ashes for a week. Tie them up in your smokehouse and smoke them with very green hickory chips for a period of six weeks. After smoking, the hams can be stored in hickory ashes, completely covered.

To smoke fish, salt it down, then smoke it. The smoking should be *continuous* on fish: four to six days of uninterrupted smoke. The continuous smoking is to prevent spoiling—smoking fish is usually done in the summer.

Right now, you can still receive bulletins from the county extension agent as well as some how-to-do-it material from salt companies on curing and butchering, etc. Sugar cure is also available at some stores now. Start doing this and working out your own recipes.

14-TANNING

Tanning is the preserving of hides for leather for coats, shoes, mittens, mufflers, purses, boots, and many other things. We'll be using the hides of goats, rabbits, hogs, sheep, and an occasional deer.

Sheepskin happened to be my easiest experience, although "easy" has nothing to do with tanning. Tanning is pure, hard work. I tried to find a method to tan without using anything from the store, and guess what? The Indians have been doing it for years. We found an Indian method that calls for a pole, maybe six inches in diameter, with a seat made on it. The pole is laid at a 45° angle, and the fibers of the hide are broken by pulling the hide again and again over the smooth, rounded surface. These dried, broken fibers are worked and worked over the pole. As these fibers are dried and broken, the hide is rubbed with oil. This is the method we are eventually going to use. Our oil will come from our sunflowers.

Another method is called alum-salt process, good for smaller hides. Again, when you run out of alum and salt, you're going to have to work this out. Tannic acid, extracted from acorns, oak bark, and the bubbles on the oak leaves, can be substituted for the alum. (Refer to Chapter 1 on extraction.)

The first thing of course is to carefully skin the animal; make sure that you don't tear any holes in the hide. Secure the skin, and remove all the fleshy pieces and fat from the hide with a *dull* knife.

After you have removed all the flesh from the hide, embed the hide with salt, and put it in a cool place for one to two days. Then start working on it again by scraping off the excess flesh or fat that the salt has loosened. Soak the hide in a mixture of one part salt to four parts water in a crock or wooden barrel. (Don't use metal!) Soak it in this solution one day for small skins, or two to three weeks for large hides. After you get them in the salt solution, you can more or less work the hide at your will.

Take the hides from the container and wring them out. Put the hide back in the container and cover completely with a solution of one cup alum, three cups salt, and eight cups water. Stir the hide twice a day for at least a week or ten days. This soaks the hide completely with alum and salt. I had trouble with the hide floating to the top, so I used a big dish, weighted with a stone atop it, to hold the hide down.

After seven to ten days, remove the hide and place it under running water. Wash thoroughly for at least a half hour or until the hide is not salty. The best way to tell if there's any salt on it is to put your tongue against the hide and taste it. Put the hide out in the sunshine on a pole or the clothesline. Stretch it out and make sure that it dries completely. It must be kept out in the sun until it is dried; if you leave it inside, it will rot. The hide on the clothesline or pole will get white and stiff. Then you start pulling and stretching and working the hide between your hands. For small hides, break over a rounded surface such as a table edge. Make sure that this is done completely.

To make the hide more pliable you can use neatsfoot oil, if you can get it, or vaseline. We're going to try using our sunflower oil instead. Start with small quantities and work the oil into your hide until it is very pliable. I'd say this is how the Indians made the brown buckskin.

Finally, build yourself a small rack and stretch your hide over it with the fur side up and build a smoke under it. Smoking gives the hide a definite preserving and water-shedding quality. You can smoke it until it turns from buckskin to black.

In our research to find a good recipe for tanning, again the Indians had a good idea. The reason the Blackfoot Indians were called Blackfoot is because they made their moccasins from the smoke flaps of their tents.

15-HORSE

Like any girl who has grown up watching doe-eyed cowgirls swept off their horses by strong-armed men in white, I've always wanted a horse of my own. The man of my dreams has strong arms, but his ideas of a horse to plow the garden dampened mine of a tall, slender-legged, chestnut steed. Fortunately, the Lord had the perfect horse in mind, and brought our attention to Stormy.

Larry Carey, a good friend in Faith Assembly, the church that meets in the Barn, mentioned that he had a half-Arabian horse for sale. Not knowing what an Arabian was all about, we went to see him. Three identical (to us) horses walked into the barn. One with big gentle brown eyes came over to check us out. He was very tall, and had a massive chest and head. Larry said he was a dotey, good-looking horse that needed some work. I thought Stormy was fantastic. Mel thought a dotey, slow horse would be good to learn on, and that chest looked like it would pull anything. Stormy was "green broke," and hadn't been ridden much for two or three years.

Well, I was right. He is fantastic . . . fantastically stubborn, strong-willed, and smart. Larry was right, too. Stormy is good-looking, and did he need work! But Larry was wrong about one thing. That horse loves to trot, he loves to canter, and he loves to run. Most of all, he likes to run riderless. Mel was ready to get rid of him, yet we knew he was from the Lord, so we persisted.

Horses have very good memories, so you have to be consistent, and you can't let them get away with one thing. Twice we had to battle Stormy for two hours to get the bit in his mouth. We took him out to ride three days after we got him. Although he had been cooperating beautifully, this day he decided enough was enough. He pulled back so hard that he broke the halter. After a great deal of trouble, we finally learned to close off his air by pressing down on either side of his nose just above his nostrils. Now he voluntarily opens his mouth for the bit.

We had some problems staking him out. He's so strong that he either broke the rope or pulled up the stakes. We didn't have our pasture fenced in when we got him, and one time we caught him trotting across the parking lot, dragging a 50-pound block of cement as if it wasn't there. In desperation we went to a local tack shop and the man sold us a chain which weaves up through the bottom ring on his nylon halter, across his nose, and up to his ear ring. The bottom of the chain is hooked to his rope, and the chain effectively cuts off his wind if he jerks on it.

Since we have a tractor in use, we haven't had to teach him to plow, but we will begin his training shortly. We will start by teaching him to pull a one-horse garden plow or sleigh.

Taking care of the horse is easy. The amount of feed given depends on the size of the horse. We feed Stormy two quarts of oats and seven pounds of hay twice a day. When he works, he will be fed three times. He is pastured during the day in the summer; if the pasture is thick enough, the hay is eliminated. A horse will drink twelve to twenty gallons of water daily.

For his health, and to keep him obedient, a horse should be exercised twenty minutes each day unless he is being worked. To exercise or "gyp" a horse, find a level spot of ground with room enough to run the horse in circles with a radius of the length of a long lead rope. Ours is fifteen-twenty feet long. Keep off to his side, but close to his rear, and snap him with the rope. Have him trot in circles around you; go through the commands. Tell him how good he is, then send him in circles the other way. You are keeping your horse in good condition and teaching him to obey you at the same time. Horses that are stabled constantly because of lack of pasture space or weather conditions *have* to be exercised every day. Otherwise, there will be a build-up of fluid in their feet and legs. When we first tried to gyp Stormy, he broke and ran. So we stood by a stake and when he broke, wrapped our end of the rope around the stake. He got an abrupt jerk on his nose, and after a couple of these lessons, he never broke again. You will spend about half an hour a day caring for your horse, which isn't bad for all the pleasure he gives!

We bed Stormy with straw, pine needles, sawdust, leaves, or anything that's dry and available. The horse's stall should be cleaned out periodically. (Who likes to sleep in a mess?!) You'll find his bedding to be one of the best fertilizers around. Since his steel shoes pulverize it, the bedding decomposes quickly.

Stormy is a typical male in the prime of his life, and doesn't like to be told what to do. He's also a lovable boy who likes to show off his affection by rubbing his head against you, or nibbling at you with his lips. We know he's perfect for us, because he's from the Lord.

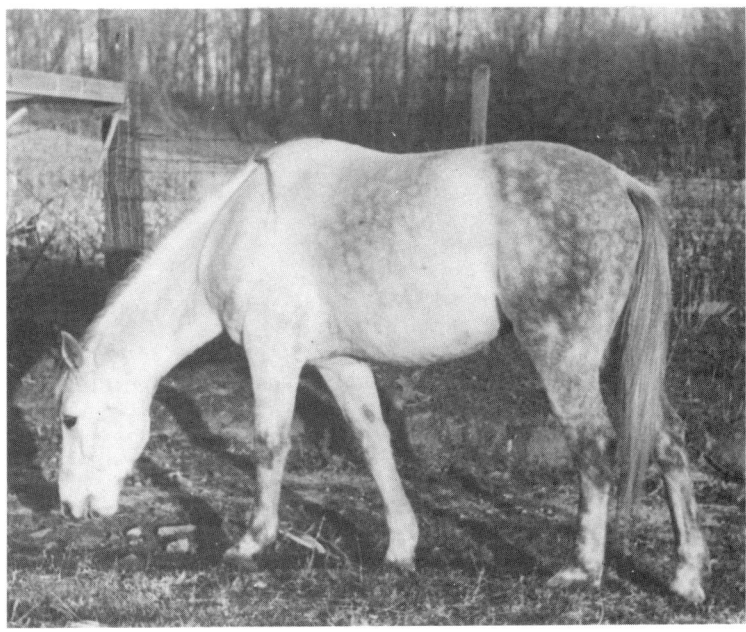

16-GOATS

"And thou shalt have goats' milk enough for thy food, for the food of thy household, and for the maintenance for thy maidens" —Prov. 27:27

"Goats' milk, Mel?" asked one of the girls from New Life Community in Michigan.

"Sure," Mel took the glass she offered and handed it to Merrybeth to see if she'd make a face.

Mel tried the milk . . . *after* Merrybeth tasted it. They were both surprised to find that it tasted similar to cows' milk, but a little richer.

When Mel and Merrybeth returned from Michigan and told Steve and me about the milk, our reactions were just about the same: "Goats' milk!?"

Well, we bought some milk goats. We read that there were five main breeds of dairy goats: French Alpine, Toggenburg, American LaMancha, Nubian, and Saanen. We bought a grade Nubian and a grade Saanen for $40 each. Our Nubian was pregnant and already dry, and our Saanen was pregnant, but still milking.

The price that we gave for these goats was really from the Lord. After looking around for quite a while, we soon discovered that milk goats are not cheap. A registered goat usually starts at $175 or $200 apiece. We will be improving the quality of our stock by breeding and obtaining better quality animals. You may wonder, "Why not buy a cow?" Goats are more practical, since one cow eats as much grain and hay as eight goats. That's quite a savings!

It is important to check the udder, teats, and taste the milk before purchasing your goat. The udder should be large, even, and pliable, not meaty or hard. The teats should be even and easy to hold, but not too big.

Goats are sensitive, easily upset animals. If there's any disturbance in the barn, they may draw the milk back into their udder. However, a goat can be very stubborn, so show her who's boss from the start.

After purchasing your goat, you may find that her milking capacity is not even close to what the owner said it would be. Don't be disappointed, though. Moving a goat from one home to another will upset her. Be patient and gentle, let her get used to you and her new surroundings. She'll work herself back up again.

Our experience with goats has been humorous, rewarding, fun, and faith-filled. When we first got our goats, none of us knew how to milk. Steve was elected to try first, but nothing happened. Then Mel tried and got some milk.

Milking can be very enjoyable, but there is a technique. The goat will stand very still if you give her her grain at milking time. This keeps her mind off the milking, and gets her fed at the same time. Our milking stand has been very useful and worth the time to build. Mel looked at quite a few of them before he came up with this one:

How do you milk?

After washing the udder with warm, soapy water, take one teat in each hand. Holding the top of the teat with thumb and index finger so the milk doesn't go back into her udder, close one finger at a time—middle, ring and pinky—in a downward motion to extract the milk. The first squirt from each teat should not go in your milking pail as it cleans the nipple from dirt. Make sure the goat is milked dry. After she has given all you think she's got, massage her udder. This relaxes her muscles a little more. Milk again, she will give a little more. At the very last of the milking, the teats will need to be "stripped," a technique done with the thumb and index finger. Simply keep these fingers tight, and slowly pull down toward the end of the teat until there's no more milk.

The milk absorbs odor very quickly, so strain it through a cloth and store in a refrigerator as soon as possible. The straining eliminates any hair or straw that may have fallen into the milk. It is also a good idea to clip the hair off the udder, which will further reduce the hair and dirt. Some goats give as much as a gallon of milk a day. It is very important to keep a feeding and milking schedule; twelve hour intervals are best.

Our goats are fed a mixture of corn and oats, and all the hay they will eat. A good recipe for fifty pounds of goat feed is:

    35 lbs. oats
    10 lbs. barley or bran
    5 lbs. cracked corn

This should be thickened with three pounds of blackstrap molasses, if it's available. One or two pounds of trace mineral should be added. One quart of the corn-oats mixture per feeding per goat is recommended. A salt block should be provided at all times.

To make a good hay feeder, use a 55-gallon drum. Three openings 8 inches wide, 12 inches high and 10 inches off the ground should be cut in the side for the goats to feed through. This feeder enables you to drop a whole bale of hay in, remove the strings, and replace the lid, keeping the hay dry and cutting waste and leaf loss. During the summer, the goats are turned out to pasture, but still given grain at milking time. Fresh water twice daily is given: cold water in the warm months, and warm water in the cold months.

Goats kept in a warm barn don't wear off the hoof material as do goats raised in mountainous, cliffy areas. Therefore, it is necessary to clean and trim the hooves of the goats. Check them once a month to see if they need to be trimmed. A knife or pruning shears is recommended for this. Always work away from yourself and the goat. Place the hoof between your knees, and trim a thin slice at a time. Stop trimming at the first sight of pink. Trim the heel so the goat can stand level.

If you intend to breed your own goats, make sure the billy is housed at least seventy-five feet from the milking area. The billy has a strong, offensive odor, and it is not advisable for small farm owners to keep a billy for this reason. The odor can be eliminated somewhat by keeping the billy's long hair trimmed, giving him a bath regularly, and thoroughly cleaning his stall at least once every two weeks. Steve suggested that if you start the baths at a very early age, the billy might even come up to your house and say, "Baaaaaaaaath!"

Does carry their kids—one to five at a time—for twenty-one to twenty-three weeks. Stagger the breeding of your does so you will have milk year around. The doe usually dries up about two months before freshening (giving birth). About a week before freshening, separate the doe from the rest of the herd, and put her in a clean, well-bedded, draft-free pen. After the doe freshens, help her clean off the kids. Separate the kids from the doe three to five days after birth, to keep the nursing from harming the teats. The young kids should then be fed eight ounces of milk per kid from bottles four times daily. If available, you might want to use a milk supplement. The doe's milk has colostrum, which has a lot of vitamins and extra nourishment the kids need, for about ten days after birth. Therefore, this milk should be consumed only by the kids.

If you plan to butcher the billy kids, it is preferable to castrate them (within ten days after birth) or the meat will have a taint to it. To castrate, cut off one-third of the scrotum with a sharp knife that has been boiled. After forcing the testicles out, pull the attached cords steadily. Cut the cords and clean the wound. Another method of castration is the elastrator (rubber band).

After castration, the billies are called wethers. They should be turned out to pasture for the summer, and then put on grain and kept in a fattening pen thirty to forty days before butchering. Chevon (goat meat) is very tasty and should be prepared as lamb is.

Billy kids kept for breeding should be separated from the doe kids at four months of age, as they will breed too early, and stunt the doe's growth. The does shouldn't be bred until they're twelve to eighteen months old.

The Lord gave goats horns as a defensive device. However, if you find the goats butting each other and meaning business, it may be wise to dehorn them. The best method is to use a saw to cut a ring all around the base of the horn. Place an elastrator band or tight rubber band in the ring, tape it over so the band doesn't slip off. It will take six to eight weeks for the horns to fall off. This is the least trouble for you and the least traumatic for the goat.

Before learning of this method of dehorning, we had some trouble with our Saanen butting our new grade Nubian. The new goat wouldn't fight, but would just stick her head behind the gate and refuse to eat. We finally decided to dehorn the Saanen. Using a hacksaw, it took about five minutes to cut off her horns. She came back into the barn looking rather peaked; her eyes had lost color, and she didn't look too happy. At the next milking, we discovered she had a very high fever, and when we milked her we got blood. We rebuked whatever it was that she had in the name of Jesus, and asked Him to heal her. Jesus said, "If ye shall ask anything in my name, I will do it" (John 14:13).

We knew by faith it was done. A couple of days later, we talked to a Spirit-filled veterinarian and asked him what exactly she had. He said it was gangrene, and to rebuke it. We rebuked the gangrene in Jesus' name, and two days later, the manifestation was already noticeable.

17-BUTTER & CHEESE

We use goat milk for making butter and cheese. When we prepare to make butter, we let the milk set in a cool place for twenty-four hours, and then skim the cream off. This cream is kept in a quart jar until the jar was about one-half full, and then shaken continuously for about forty-five minutes. We pour off the excess liquid which makes buttermilk when thoroughly cooled and soured. The remaining butter is soft and white. After removing the butter from the jar, we place it in a bowl and wash it. We add a little water to the butter, and, using a spoon, fold the butter gently until the water becomes clear. We pour off the water and repeat. Finally, we add salt to taste.

We haven't made cheese yet, but I'd like to give you two of the recipes we'll be using.

Unheated Cottage Cheese:
    1 gallon raw milk
    1 cup sour cream

Sour Cream

Combine 1 T. vinegar or lemon juice with one cup cream. Combine raw milk and sour cream and let stand at room temperature until thick. Refrigerate until mixture is cooled, and then put in a cheesebag or cloth-lined colander to drip and let stand for 48 hours. Remove from bag and refrigerate. This is softer than store-bought cottage cheese. For your next culture, you can use one cup of the thickened milk instead of sour cream. Save the whey that drips from the colander for a cold drink.

The following recipes are from one of our friends from old Mexico. She has a lot of experience with cheese-making, butter-making, butchering, barbequing, and homemade rennet (recipe following).

Rennet can be made from the stomach of a baby goat that is not more than two or three weeks old and is only on mother's milk. Remove the second stomach, tying one end closed, pouring in a lot of salt, then tying the other end closed. In Mexico, these stomachs are hung in the sun to dry, but you may want to use your oven on *low* heat. When dried, the inside of the stomach will be a dried powder.

To make a quart of rennet, 2 T. of this dried powder is added to one quart of water. Store in refrigerator until ready for use. If refrigeration is not available, make smaller amounts.

Soft Cheese:
    1 rennet tablet
    2 T. salt
    1 cup warm water
    1 gallon raw milk

Dissolve salt and rennet in water, add to milk and let it set at room temperature until it gels. Cut gel in squares with a knife. Let this set for one hour or until the water comes to the top, and the cheese is on the bottom. Put in a cheesecloth bag, and squeeze juice off. Add more salt to taste. Remove from cheesecloth and shape into patties. This is ready to eat now, and may be stored in refrigerator.

18-PIGEONS

When praying about what animals to keep on our farm, the Lord impressed upon us to get pigeons. They are as prolific as rabbits.

The local county agent gave Steve and me the address of a man in the county who raised Giant Ruts. When we got there, we were really surprised at the size of these birds—between three and four pounds. This breeder gave us the name of two other breeders who might let us see how they had set up their pigeon fly. One raised Kings pigeons which I had read about and was becoming partial to. The other, Glen Voris, raised only showbirds and homers. I took the address of the man with the Kings and through this man's insistance, reluctantly went to see Mr. Voris.

When we arrived, we told him that we just wanted to see his pigeon fly to know how to set ours up. We witnessed to him about Christ and the work here at the Barn.

While he was showing us around, he said, "Now, exactly how many of these birds are you ready to take?"

"We don't believe you understand," we said. "We

don't have any money today, and we were just interested in your buildings."

He went on as if he didn't hear us. "I will give you one pair, two pairs, or any amount of these show and breeding birds you want."

Mel asked him to explain "give;" Mr. Voris replied, "I mean 'give'."

Steve and I told him we would be back on Tuesday. We rushed home and immediately started to construct our pigeon fly.

Some of these birds were in the $100 show category. We took eleven of Mr. Voris' birds, and sent to Florida for five pairs of Kings.

We didn't have any success breeding the pigeons until the Lord sent us Bruce, who has been taking care of and spending a lot of time with the birds. The following paragraphs are Bruce's contribution to this book.

Pigeons are more than just some bird you see flying around in the city. They are very productive and good for eating if properly cared for. Without good care, pigeons are almost worthless, so some basic ideas on caring for them are necessary.

First, of course, provide a place for them to live. We have a fairly small flock of ten to fifteen birds. The area we keep them in is about nine foot by nine foot with standing room; this makes it easy to work with the flock. If the pen is kept clean, with an ample supply of food and water, the flock will fly in and out without leaving permanently.

Nests are necessary to the cote. Two boxes for each mated pair provides a place for the adult birds to nest and also a place for squabs (young pigeons). These nests should be about the size of an orange crate with a partition in the middle. Across the front, a perch and small wall approximately four inches high should be built so the eggs won't fall out.

Keep the bedding fresh—hay or straw is best. Roosts should be available for the pigeons. We made ours by stacking crates end on end with a board sticking out of each one a few inches for the bird to sit on.

Pigeons need and like baths. Put a tub of water in the pen for a few hours once a week.

Pigeons should have a good supply of fresh food and water at all times. We have been using regular chicken laying mash for our breeders along with a few crushed egg shells. When we can't buy or sell, we will be feeding our birds our own homemade laying mash, supplemented with sunflower seeds, cracked corn, and cowpeas.

Once a pigeon finds a mate, the two will stay together for life unless forcibly broken up. Sometimes one male will take two hens. This should be remedied by getting a single cock to take one of the hens.

Laying and hatching should be watched closely and proper records must be kept. The hen will usually lay two eggs at an interval of about forty to forty four hours. Both eggs will hatch, if fertile, about seventeen to eighteen days later. Seven to eleven days after the eggs have been laid, the eggs should be candled. This is done by holding the egg up to a bright light. Look for blood vessels and a dark center, which indicates that the squab is starting to form. If the bird has not started to form at eleven days, the egg should be destroyed so that the hen can lay more eggs.

On the eighteenth day, unhatched eggs should be checked again. If there is a squab in the egg, you may

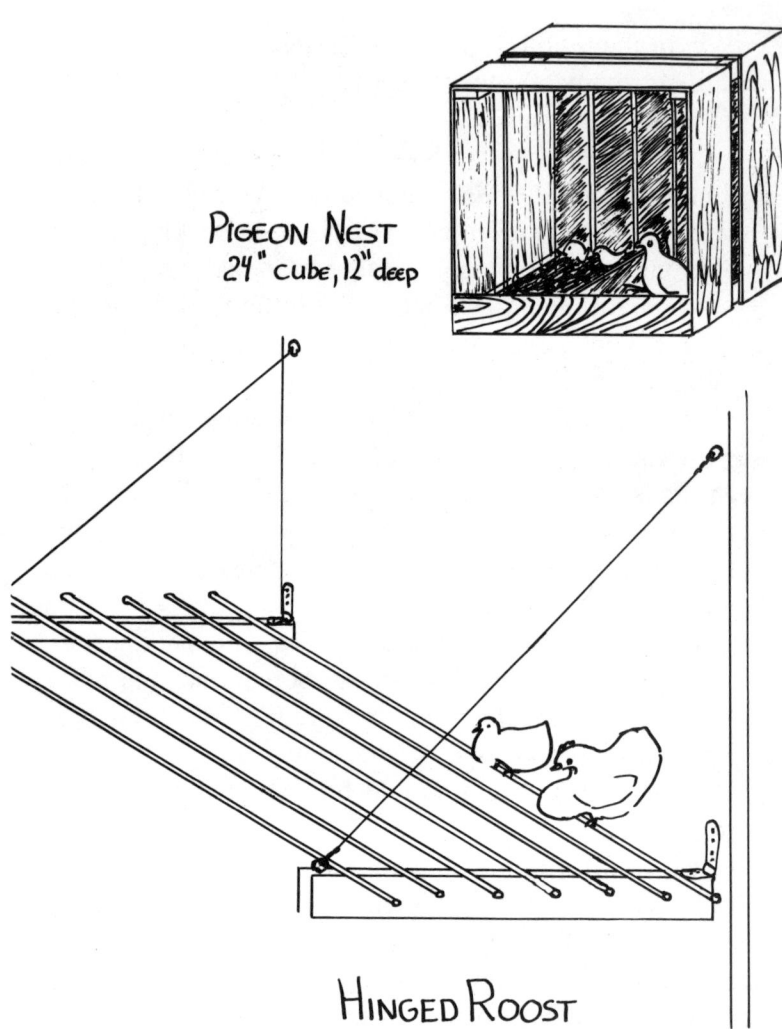

need to break open the end and help the squab's head out. Seventy-five percent of all eggs laid will probably be fertile.

A squab's growth is very rapid. Within seven days, feathers are present. On the tenth day, banding is necessary to distinguish the birds. On the twenty-fourth day, the bird is ready for butchering or separation from the rest of the flock so it won't break up any mated pairs.

Molting—when a bird sheds old feathers to grow new ones—occurs at about six weeks of age and from then on, annually.

Sometimes mates lose their sex instinct and the hen's eggs, of course, will be infertile. This may mean the pen needs a good cleaning or painting. Sometimes separation of the cock from the hen for a few days will work. After separating the pair, put the cock in a pen where the hen can see him. This will create a new desire for each other. The male will strut, fan his tail, and puff up his chest. When this happens, he should be banded and returned to his mate.

A lot of prayer was necessary for our pigeons, like anything else, so that action should be Number One.

19-HOGS

Although Mel had yielded to the fact that the Lord wanted to use the place as a farm, he said he would *never* raise hogs because of the smell. One day while at a blacksmith and repair shop getting our wagon fixed, Mel looked at the blacksmith's hogs and asked him if he ever had any runts.

He replied, "Yes, would you like a couple?"

Mel has now learned to never say never. He returned home that day with two small pigs.

A lot of farmers will give away runts because they don't want to take the time to raise them up. The larger hogs push them away from the food and water, and eventually the runt may die.

We built a small pen out of gates for our pigs, and put an old chicken brooder over them for shelter.

We found that pigs eat just about anything. You can grow your own feed, such as corn, sorghum, barley, wheat, rye, and oats. They also like meals made from soybean oil, linseed oil, cottonseeds, peanuts, fish, meat scraps, skim milk, and tankage (a feed made from bones, tendons, and other parts of animals). When we butchered our chickens, we gave our pigs the entrails, heads, and feet—they really thought they were getting a feast!

Pigs also need minerals such as salt, and pasture crops like alfalfa for vitamins.

The pig doesn't have to be entirely grain-fed, but if you're given a hog that has had nothing but grain, don't change its diet overnight. Continue to feed it grain in decreasing amounts as you gradually increase the scraps.

Our pigs are a living garbage disposal. We give them all our scraps except the bones.

The young pig should be fed three times daily. This can be changed to twice after the pig is six weeks old. Fresh water should be available at all times. The pig will also eat garden wastes such as cabbage, brussel sprouts, kale, cauliflower, pea and bean vines, roasting ears. They especially like potatoes, grass clippings, and fruits.

A small "pig garden" can be planted with Jerusalem artichokes, sugar beets, carrots, potatoes, corn and soybeans. They also like skim milk, bakery wastes, eggplant, and acorns.

When the old-timers had a hog kill, two or three families would get together and kill ten to twenty hogs at a time. It's good to have extra hands when butchering. You'll probably have people in the area who were involved in this when they were children; they are really helpful.

Two extra blessings of butchered hogs are lard and cracklings. The old way to render lard was to build a tripod, hang an old iron kettle on it over an outside fire, and put in the excess fat from the hog. The fat will almost disintegrate and turn to liquid. Dip off the clear liquid, and put in containers to cool.

Cracklings are the fat and the hide. The hide, with a thin layer of fat, has to be boiled and scraped, and the hair removed before you can make cracklings. To make cracklings, cut the clean hide in small pieces, drop them in the fat when you are rendering down your lard, and boil it briskly. About the time they start to turn brown, reduce the heat a little. They will sink to the bottom, so dip them off the bottom with a ladle. Put them in a sausage press to remove the excess fat. These are very good for "munchies" by the fire. (For curing instructions, refer to Chapter 13.)

20-RABBITS

Being a city girl, private secretary, and sheltered Christian, I had never known that people actually ate rabbit, let alone raised rabbits for anything besides pets. But here at the Glory Barn, eyes are opened, and the scripture in 1 Timothy 4:4 takes on new meaning. It says that nothing is to be refused if it is received with thanksgiving.

The Lord told us to raise rabbits because they reproduce quickly and abundantly. We did some research and thought we would like to raise Californians, a medium-sized rabbit raised for meat. Some friends in Faith Assembly gave us Benjamin—a Californian buck—complete with hutch. Then other friends who hadn't had much success raising rabbits gave us a Checkered Giant and a Flemish Giant doe. We were off into the rabbit business.

We found a young, bred Californian doe at Harold Wolf's Rabbitry a few miles from here. She had twelve bunnies in her first litter, but because of her youth and our ignorance, we lost them all. Her litter was to be our basic breeding stock, and we were pretty discouraged.

Mr. Wolf said he would re-breed her right away, and in the meantime, our checkered Giant had kindled (given birth to) seven young, and we lost only one.

The first thing we had to consider was housing for the rabbits. We started with outdoor housing because we had no place to shelter them. We used wire cages with wooden hutches on the back. The hutch provided shelter in bad weather, and the wire fronts a place to exercise and cool. The wooden-floored hutches are hard to keep clean because there is no place for the waste to go. In the wire cages, it falls through to the ground, and so they are almost self-cleaning.

We always take the doe to the buck's hutch for mating, because she will not attack in strange places—he will. (Never house two bucks together as they will fight.) After they have mated, she is returned to her hutch and re-bred again three days later. A doe shows signs of being ready to mate by restlessness and rubbing. But she can be bred whether she's showing these signs or not. If she starts making a nest eighteen-twenty days later, suspect false pregnancy and re-breed right away.

Twenty-seven days after a doe is bred, we put a nesting box lined with clean straw or hay in her hutch. She will pull fur from her chest and make a nest for her litter. A nesting box is a sturdy box completely closed-in except for an entrance and exit hole. The opening should be three to four inches above the bottom of the box so that the young cannot come out before they are ready.

We work with the does, expecially when it is time to kindle. Does are very protective of their young, and they will cannibalize if they fear for their young. We talk to them, pet them, and check the nesting box every time we are around. That way they are used to us and unafraid.

The litter will be born from twenty-nine to thirty-five days after breeding. A day after kindling, check the litter to see how many there are, and make sure they are in one bunch in the nest. We try to breed our does so that they kindle at the same time. That way some of a large litter can be moved to a smaller litter three or four days after kindling. California's second litter had ten bunnies. Two were runts and by the third day they were starving. We took three of her largest bunnies and put them in with Fleming's five (who were huge). For several days we held the runts to the mother twice a day to nurse. After that, they were strong enough to nurse themselves. A doe will nurse her young for about eight weeks.

The young's eyes will open ten days after birth. Check them, and if one or two eyes are shut, wash them out with warm water and a clean cloth. Nineteen or twenty days after kindling, the bunnies will come out of their nest. If they come out before that, put them back, because their mother won't, and she won't nurse a split litter.

We feed our rabbits as much hay as they will eat, a half cup of pellets, and fresh water in the morning and at night. When the doe has kindled, she and her litter get as many pellets as they will eat, and fresh water all the time.

After we cannot buy pellets, we will feed them oats, buckwheat, and milled corn for the grain. Some table wastes can be fed—lettuce, bread, carrots, turnips, and beets can be supplemental feed. We have to watch our breeding stock to make sure they don't get too fat, because overweight bucks and does produce small litters.

Salt is necessary to their diet, so we put salt spools in their hutches. You can add a touch of salt to their food daily.

Rabbits hop around a lot, so heavy crocks for food and water are essential to prevent tipping. If these aren't available, old coffee cans cut down and sharp edges bent over are good. Plastic containers do not last too long, because rabbits nibble on everything.

Middle-weight does like ours can be bred at five to six months, and the bucks at six to seven months. A good doe can produce four litters a year. Six weeks after a doe gives birth, she can be bred again, and still have two weeks alone to settle her nerves before the next litter arrives. Just make sure your breeding schedule isn't ahead of your housing. All those rabbits have to have a place to live after they are weaned.

We are working on a quonset hut right now to house our rabbits. When it is done, they will all be in wire hutches. We will be putting them in double deck form, and will have to place a piece of metal below the second row. It will be slanted so the wastes roll off the back onto the ground.

After you have a sizable herd, hutch cards and records are necessary for proper breeding and production efficiency.

The rabbits must have heard God tell Adam and Eve to be fruitful and multiply. We haven't checked their fruits, but they sure have multiplied! In six months, thirty-four bunnies have been born, and that's a lot of meat. Hallelujah!

21-CHICKENS

In August, Tip, who recently accepted Christ, told us that his father would possibly give us a start of laying chickens. We said, "Praise the Lord! But now what?" Soon after that news, another brother had to move from a chicken farm and had excess feed to give us. With twenty laying hens and feed, all we needed to do was put a few patches on the chicken house and we were ready to go.

We already had a chicken house which was divided into two rooms. The smaller room is used for the baby chicks until they are about eight weeks old. A small door is provided for them so they can get outside and range. The larger room is for the laying hens; a door is also provided for them to go outside. A fenced-in yard in front of the chicken house enables the chickens to range without danger from predators.

One of the first things we discovered is that a folding roost is a must for cleaning in the chicken house. This roost is on hinges and can be fastened to the wall when hauling manure out of the coop. We put the manure on our garden since it is high in nitrogen.

Good maintenance in the chicken house is also necessary. The nests need to be partitioned. Our nests are sixteen inches high, twelve inches wide, and thirteen inches deep. The nests also need to have clean straw at all times.

In February, we bought 100 White Rock chicks for $27.50. White Rocks are a breed good for both meat and eggs. We kept our chicks under a thermostat-controlled electric brooder. Heat lamps can also be used, but are not advisable as they may start fires and are hard to keep at the right temperature. For the first week, the heat should be kept between 85° and 90°. This temperature is warm enough so the chicks won't gather around the heat and smother each other, and cool enough that they won't get away from the heat and freeze. Each week after the first, the heat should be reduced 5° until the temperature is 65°. At this time the brooder can be removed. Litter, sawdust, wood shavings, pine needles, straw, should be on the floor and kept stirred to prevent caking. If caking occurs, remove the caked litter from the house and put on your garden or compost pile. Water and fresh, dry feed should be available to them at all times. Chick starter feed can be bought at a feed mill.

You may be wondering why we didn't use an incubator and hatch our own baby chicks instead of buying them. We did try one, but had very poor results. We put thirty eggs in the incubator, turned them three times a day, and kept water in the pan so they wouldn't dry out. After the required twenty-one days, only three of the eggs had hatched. We decided that next time we would set our hens.

To set hens, separate an older hen who shows signs of wanting to set from the rest of the chickens; give her ten to twelve eggs. The eggs should hatch within twenty-one days. You won't need chick starter, because the chicks will follow the hen around to eat what she eats. You won't need brooders either, because the chicks will stay under the hen's wings for warmth and security. As the hen is to her chicks, the Lord is to us: "He shall cover thee with His feathers, and under His wings shalt thou trust; his truth shall be thy shield and buckler" (Ps. 91:4).

We decided this is the natural way which is the best way to hatch chicks, since this is how God planned it. The chicks and setting hen can be put back with the rest of the chickens when the chicks are between six to eight weeks old. If done before this, the other chickens may kill the chicks.

Young chickens six to thirteen weeks old are used for broiling and frying, four-to six-month-old chickens are for roasting, and chickens older than six months for stewing. A hen is ready for laying and breeding at twenty to twenty-three weeks of age and may lay 200 eggs a year. During the molting season in the fall, however, the egg production may slacken. After we harvest this fall, our chickens will be fed a fifty percent corn-fifty percent oats mixture, and all of the leafy hay they will eat. Egg shells can be ground through the meat grinder and recycled through the feed to add calcium to their diet.

The eggs can be used right away, or can be made into noodles.

Noodles:
>   1 pint egg yolks
>   1 pint water
>   flour (enough to knead and roll out)
>   salt to taste

Combine above ingredients. Roll out thin. Let dry until the top is not damp. Toss over so underneath side gets dry, too. Cut into noodles and let dry at least one day before storing. Any moisture in the noodles will make them mold. Store in air-tight containers.

The egg whites can be used for "angel food" cakes, but that is another story.

Cleaning chickens is not a "fun" process, but it is necessary if you want to eat your chickens. Using baler twine or any kind of strong string, tie the chicken by its feet and let it hang. Chop its head off with a sharp knife or ax and let the body bleed four or five minutes. Then dip the chicken into a pail of *boiling* water, making sure all feathers are fully immersed. Now, pluck the feathers. There will be a few hairs left on the bird, which can be easily removed by building a small fire and singeing them off. Pin feathers should be removed by plucking. Remove the oil gland from the topside of the tail.

Laying the chicken on its back, carefully cut a slit from the anus to the tip of the breastbone. Remove the insides of the chicken by putting your hand in the slit, pulling insides out, making sure all internal organs are removed. With your index finger scrape the chicken along the rib cage to remove the pink lungs. If done correctly, the liver, heart and gizzard will come out unharmed. Cut the gizzard along the seam, remove contents and the yellowish skin. Wash well, and place chicken, liver, heart, and gizzard in cold salted water until ready for use.

There are five steps to cutting up a chicken. (1) Chill the chicken for twelve hours. (2) Cut the wings off. (3) Pull the leg apart from the body so that the joint is easily seen to remove the legs. (4) Run the knife through both sides of the rib cage as close as possible to the back. This is easily done, as there is an area free of bones here. (5) Pull it apart with your hands, having back in one hand and breast in the other.

Now your chicken is cut and ready for frying, stewing, canning, or broiling. (For canning instructions, refer to Chapter 8.)

As the Lord gave us an abundance, we were able to bless someone else with six hens and a rooster, which will enable them to start their own egg factory and meat supply.

22-BEES

"Ye shall inherit their land, and I will give it unto you to possess it, a land that floweth with milk and honey"—Lev. 20:24

We knew the Lord was leading us to have bees on our farm, but we didn't know where to start. On the way from Fort Wayne one day, the Lord led us to stop at a field where a man was working with bees. Mr. Delp turned out to be a Christian who was interested in helping people get started with bees. We've found that bee people are really nice, in love with their bees, and wanting to get others excited about honeybees. Mr. Delp said he would help us get started and give us one hive with bees and brood chamber honey, four empty hives (two with brood chamber honey), a helmet, veil, gloves, a smoker to calm the bees down, and a lot of information all for $35. That was from the Lord! All we would have to do is buy bees for four hives.

What worried us was the foreign terminology: foundations, brood chambers, queen excluders, supers, smokers, caps, hives, swarms, hive tools, fume boards, feeders. We read *How to Keep Bees and Sell Honey* published by the Walter T. Kelley Company of Clarkson, Kentucky. This book has the information for everything you will need. Your county agent is a good source of information, and he will know who is raising bees in your area. We went on with Mr. Delp—a little skeptical of what we were getting into, but knowing the Lord wanted it.

You can order bees from places such as the Walter T. Kelley Co., but we found Mr. Scott, a bee supplier on 99th Street in Indianapolis, to be our man. He said that he takes care of the bees shipped to him, and we could always buy an extra queen there if we needed her. This worked out really well for us. He had slide shows of how to take the three-pound packages of bees we bought and put them into the hives.

Before trying to transfer the bees from shipping boxes into hives, we sprinkled them with sugar water to cool and calm them down. We then took out five brood chamber frames and set the box of bees down in the bottom frame. We took out the can of syrup that the bees were feeding on while being shipped, and brushed the bees into the hive. The queen and her workers were hanging on a small block of wood encased in a screen with the sugar that they were living on. We took the cork out of the end with the sugar because the other bees will accept the queen if they eat the sugar away and liberate her.

You always hear about the people who do not wear a hat and veil or gloves while working with bees. We got our bees on a cold, rainy day—the worst kind of day to try to work with bees. We were in a hurry and didn't dress right. About ten bees took advantage of the situation and flew up Mel's shirt, and stung him. Mel now dresses right. Dirk was stung on the nose, and we discovered he could really run fast. So we recommend wearing hat, veil, gloves, coveralls, and tying the pants legs shut.

One of our rewards for working with bees has been the interest of Dirk, who is thirteen. After his initial experience of being stung, he now dresses carefully and has really taken an interest in the bees. It is a good thing for Dirk and Mel to work on together.

Queen excluders keep the queen in the brood chamber. Some beekeepers use a 7-11 cut comb so that the queen won't lay eggs in the honey you're to eat. We've heard both sides, and Mr. Scott told us to do what the local people do. There may be some tricks to the trade that a man right on the spot would know about. When it is no longer possible to buy cut combs, we intend to bore two holes through the top foundation, insert a stick, bore two holes the other way, making a cross in the top chamber, and letting the bees work on the two sticks. This will be more like their habitat in the woods, and will work. Old-timers in Kentucky do beegums this way. The main thing is to get started, because if you begin in spring, you will not get any honey the following fall. The bees need what they make in summer for food in winter. The next fall, you will have honey.

We have used honey with our daughter Sundown's water since birth. It tastes good, and is good for her digestion. We use honey daily in our tea and as a sugar substitute in both cooking and baking.

Honey Kisses
    6 slices white bread, crumbled
    1 cup honey

1 cup sugar
1/2 cup butter
Heat honey, sugar and butter in a skillet until melted. Add bread crumbs and cook over low heat, stirring gently for 10 minutes. Drop by teaspoonfuls onto cookie sheet. Sprinkle with nuts if you wish. Let cool.

Honey Vinegar
1 gallon warm soft water (rain water)
2 cups clear honey
Combine ingredients. Cover, and let ferment approximately 10 days to three weeks, or to taste. It makes good vinegar.

As of yet we haven't extracted any of our own honey, but we've bought it in large quantities from Mr. Scott. You can either eat comb honey, or extract the honey by putting wire in your combs, cutting off the caps with a hot knife, and placing the combs into an extractor. The honey is spun out, and the combs are re-usable. The bees will repair these combs and make honey more quickly, so your production rate will go up. We've also heard about building a glass-covered solar wax melter that uses the sun to melt the wax. But we intend to eat comb honey and separate the wax for our candles, sewing (beeswax toughens the thread), toboggan, and other things.

We will be storing our comb honey in gallon glass jars. Mr. Scott has been trying to educate people for years to eat granulated honey. Honey granulates when stored. If you don't like the texture of granulated honey, heat it in a double boiler (not over 150° and not over an open flame) to liquify it.

Our bees are set up in our orchard so they will pollinate the trees. Some beekeepers put their hives in the shade, but this shortens their work day. We will put one or two wooden slats over the hives to give some shade in the hot months.

We were advised to grow a crop that bees could work on since there aren't enough wild flowers to support the bees. We've planted alfalfa near the bees and will let it go two weeks beyond the bloom stage. This will sacrifice some quality in the hay, but will be made up in honey production. We have also planted sunflowers, Alsike clover in our oats, and will plant buckwheat this fall, all of which provide food for the bees.

Now that we have five hives started and are assured of getting honey, we are hoping to catch bees swarming this summer. Bees swarm between May and June because they are always multiplying at this time, and the population gets too large for the hive. Somebody has to move out. If you are just beginning, however, do not start with a swarm. After you are started you can afford the time to wait for and work with a swarm.

Our honey will be our sugar, barter, and trade. We know these are the end-times and we will not be able to buy or sell unless we take the number of the anti-Christ—666. "And he causeth all, both small and great, rich and poor, free and bond, to receive a mark in their right hand, or in their foreheads; And that no man might buy or sell, save he that had the mark, or the name of the beast, or the number of his name. Here is wisdom. Let him that hath understanding count the number of the beast: for it is the number of a man; and his number is Six hundred threescore and six" (Rev. 13:16-18).

The Lord said He would give us a land of milk and honey, but we had no idea we would have to milk the goats and fight off the bees.

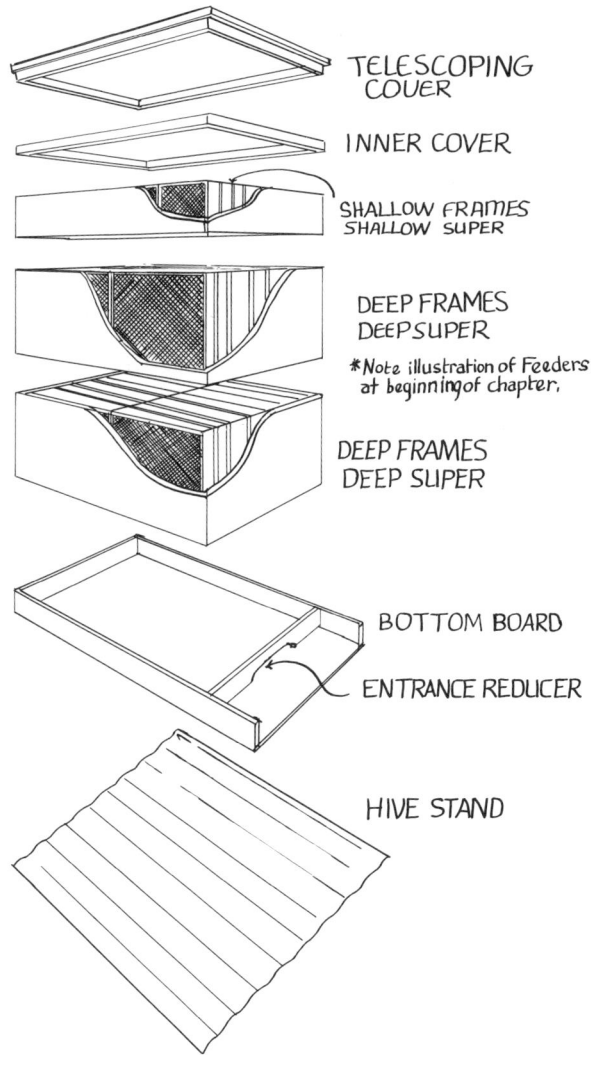

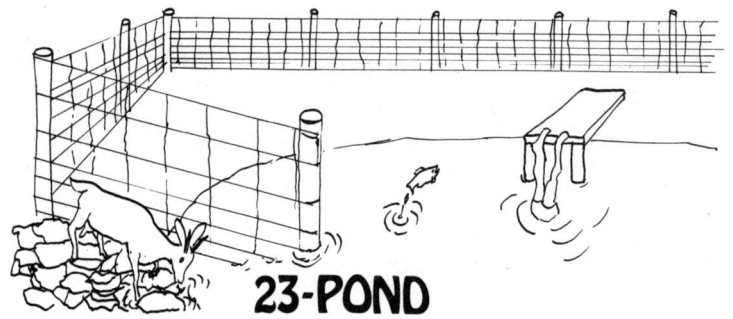

23-POND

John, a brother from our prison ministry, had offered to dig our pond. Before he arrived with the digging equipment, however, he decided to "borrow" a motor home and do a little touring. John went back to prison, and we continued to pray for the manifestation of our pond.

We called a local contractor to dig a pond for us the size of two large basements for $400. Then Jay, the contractor, uncovered an excellent top-soil and offered us $5 a load. The next deal was, he took enough top-soil to lower the cost of the pond to $200, and said if we would let him dig it larger so he could obtain more black dirt, he would hire a mobile crane to dig our pond deeper and wider.

The conclusion is that the pond, complete with drain, will cost us nothing. All the information that we could gather encourages the installation of a drain. This allows for changing of the stock and cleaning.

We thought that was the completion of our pond. Not true! So the animals won't tramp down the sides, the pond must be fenced. An eavesment must also be built out of cement or a large type gravel.

Our pond, under one acre in size, is not large enough to sustain sunfish and bass, so we will stock it with catfish. Bass, bluegill, sunfish and catfish grow very rapidly. Each body of water will produce only its own limit in pounds of fish. It is wise to consult your local division of fish and game biologists for proper stocking, how to and where to dig your pond.

After proper stocking, don't let your "friends" give you five fish of one kind and twenty-one of another. It will upset the balance of the pond. Just eat those and let your pond work naturally.

Proper care of your pond will produce tons of protein. Ponds are multipurpose. Ours will be used for baptisms, swimming, skating, food, wildlife, and watering of stock.

24-FENCE

The first job I did here at the Glory Barn was putting up a fence. A fence is a necessity if you're going to let your animals have sunlight, exercise, and fresh green pasture.

About a week after I started on the fence, Satan "lowered the boom." He was giving me lines such as, "What are you doing here instead of back at the easy factory with that nice check at the end of each week? You know that when you get this done, God will put you in another place and you'll have to do it all over again."

God allowed Satan to try me to see if I really had the desire to serve Him. Since then, I am learning that Satan just runs the same lines over and over.

Being an ex-drug addict/alcoholic with a mind not used to functioning, I'm learning how to think and care about my work. I'd have quit a long time ago if it weren't for Philippians 4:13: "I can do all things through Christ which strengtheneth me."

The best time to put a fence up is in the spring, just after the frost has left the ground. This makes it easier to work and the ground will settle and harden around the posts throughout the summer. Also, be sure to get your fence up before you get your animals.

First, count the cost; make sure there is enough fencing and posts for the area. Jesus talked about counting the cost: "For which of you, intending to build a tower, sitteth not down first, and counteth the cost, whether he have sufficient to finish it? Lest haply, after he hath laid the foundation, and is not able to finish it, all that behold it begin to mock him, Saying, This man began to build, and was not able to finish" (Luke 14:28-30).

Make sure the fence is put in right the first time by using good posts and fence and putting a final treating of creosote on the posts shortly before installation. Then decide where to put the corner posts. The fence should go on the outside around the corners, and on the inside on the lines. This prevents the staples pulling out when the animals push against the fence.

The holes for the corner posts are three feet deep. Mel asked Mr. Nei, a brother in the Body, if the posts had to be cemented in. He said no. He told us to put the posts in the center of the hole, surround the post with rocks and dirt, and tamp them down solidly. Tamp around the posts with a stick approximately one and one-half to three feet in diameter and four or five feet long, adding just enough water to the ground to pack it tight as you tamp it. Tamp about six to eight inches at one time.

As the ground settles around the corner posts after they are set, throw in some more dirt and tamp it down for about two weeks before putting the fence on. After the corner posts are good and solid, put cross-members between them so the fence will be pulling on all three posts at the corner instead of just one. The crossmembers should be put straight across and 4' high, so the goats won't climb and jump over them, then tightened with No. 9 wire.

The way to keep the line posts straight is to stretch a strand of barbed wire from corner to corner and use it as a guide for digging holes.

After having the posts all set and sturdy, it's time to stretch the fence. It is very important that it is kept tight. Mr. Nei let us use his fence stretcher.

You can put an extra strand of barbed wire on top of the posts to discourage fence-climbing.

We also needed fencing for our outside perimeter. Our fence rows were grown up and the fence was very poor. We heard that our state game preserve had planted multi-floral roses for fence, so we thought we would give it a try. It was either plant multi-floral roses or hire a bulldozer to clean out the fences completely.

We had ordered 1000 roses from the local nursery, which would cost us about $150. We had waited quite a while for them when the nursery people informed us they couldn't get us any roses. We sent to the state and asked if they had any extra.

A few days later, they called and said they had our roses. Not 1000, but 2000! My head was saying, "Where am I going to get $300?" I grabbed two extra guys and drove off thinking that we would take six trips to transport 2000 roses.

The conservation officer had the roses in two small bundles, and threw them on the truck. We asked him, "How much?" and he said these were for free. Hallelujah!

Within three years, multi-floral roses will become an

almost impenetrable living fence, which will turn even hogs. It also provides a refuge for wildlife and feeds the birds with the berries it yields.

Dr. Freeman teaching

Fruit of our labor

The log cabin

Bottling tomato juice

The fruit cellar

The friendly goats

Retreat cabin

Worshiping together

The "Glory Barn"

25-QUANSET HUT

Our quonset hut is made out of an old grain bin that had been blown down in a tornado. Some of the pieces of metal were twisted, but usable. This quonset, so far, has only cost us $15 for bolts. We will probably have $50 in the building when it is completed.

The building is eighteen feet wide by thirty feet long by ten feet high in the center. One side will be used as a rabbitry. We're getting rid of all our outside hutches, and will be using wire cages.

Under the rabbits we're going to have fishworms. These will help eliminate the rabbit manure which will provide a continuous source of food for them. We live in a lake area where we can sell bait. We figured it would be a good way for Dirk to get spending money. Later, we're going to use the fishworms in the garden to help build the soil.

The other side of the building will be used as a storage shed for our tractor and some of our machinery. Above, we will have a small loft to store hay.

Our quonset is an example of the kinds of material you can recycle. You don't have to buy or sell. You don't really have to go to the hardware, the lumber yard, or Sears and say, "I've got to have this type of building." A lot of people are trying to use different types of things for building materials. Some friends stopped by a few nights ago and told us about making buildings out of a molasses brick. We've heard of a lot of things like this. We've found that the easiest, best way is to find old buildings, old sheds, things that are falling down that people would pay you to take down. In fact, we got a lot of the material for our cabin doing this same thing. This is a good way to build a lot of the needed shelters for your animals.

26-BARN

Follow closely so you don't get confused. Our barn for the animals is not the Glory Barn which used to be for the animals, but is an old log house that was the first house built on our farm. It was moved from its original position to 200 or 300 feet away. There was a large hole cut in one side of it, and it was then used for machinery storage.

The Lord gave me an example to show that our ways are not always His ways, and our dreams are not always His will. My friend, Danny, is a very special type of guy. He can sell you anything. He'll get whatever you need, and bring you back something you don't need. Well, Danny told me he could get me a 1958 Mark III Lincoln Continental "cheap." I love old cars, but never had a chance to own one. So Danny showed me this car that was big enough for a barn dance. The lights were rusty, and I knew my wife would laugh at that, but I could just see this car finished. With about $300 it would really look good. I bought the car for $50 and became the proud owner of a Mark III Lincoln Continental. I put it in the old log house. Not too many days later, though, we bought our goats. My Lincoln Continental, my dream, was pulled out of the log house, and the log house became our barn.

Our barn is approximately eighteen by twenty-four feet with a small shed attached which we use for the goat area. We divided the barn in the middle. One-fourth of the barn with the shed on it is the goat pen. When the goats had their kids, we had set up small gates to separate them so they wouldn't bother each other. We had the milking stand and a small hay storage in another one-fourth. One-fourth of the barn belongs to Stormy, the horse. The other one-fourth is food and grain storage. Eventually we're going to install a sink.

We are using one-third of the attic for a pigeon fly. We've completely screened this part with chicken wire and put a door in. The other two-thirds of the attic is hay storage.

Another one of our friends, John, who works at a chemical company, confiscated an old leaky horse trough. Leroy and I fixed it, and it now provides an abundant supply of water for our animals in the barnyard.

The Lord sent Leroy, Sharon, and Jennifer from a charismatic body in New York. While they were here, the Lord showed them that they were to start a refuge, too. Leroy and Mel had exactly the same ideas on how to do things, but when they started a project together, their arms and legs went in different directions.

27 MIDWIFING

By thee have I been holden up from the womb; thou art he that took me out of my mother's bowels; my praise shall be continually of thee. —Ps. 71:6

When we were expecting Sundown, we made a study of the Scriptures, because "faith comes by hearing and hearing by the Word of God" (Romans 10:17). We dug in to see just what God had to say about pain, birth, and delivery, and He says a lot! Psalm 18:19, 48; 25:20; 31:1,2; 34:4,19; 37:40; 50:15; 54:7; 91:14,15 all name God as our Deliverer. There are more of these verses, but as our pastor says, "If He says it once, that's enough!" God was named as our Deliverer.

Genesis 3:16, Isaiah 13:8, and Isaiah 26:17 show that pain and sorrow were part of childbirth as a result of the curse put on woman because of Eve's disobedience to God. Pain was clearly a part of childbirth throughout the Old Testament, yet the New Testament teaches freedom from pain through Jesus' death. Christ became a curse for us to redeem us from the curse of the Law (Gal. 3:13). He suffered our pain and sorrow on the cross (Isa. 53:4; Matt. 8:17; 1 Peter 2:24). If He became a curse and suffered our pain 2,000 years ago, do we have to suffer today in childbirth? The only answer for us was no!

The Lord had given us enough scripture to go on, then He blessed us with a bonus that tied everything together. He gave us three scriptures which say that *God* takes us from the womb. Psalm 22:9; 71:6, and Isaiah 46:3 should be read by every expectant mother.

We were given natural childbirth books, but found that they ministered fear and unbelief, so we returned them. Instead of letting us be totally ignorant of the birth process, the Lord sent a few people by to tell us what to do when the baby came.

September 7 came—the baby was not due for three weeks so the contractions were mistakenly rebuked as gas pains. But we were prepared with our essentials: plastic mattress protector, scissors, boiling water, shoelaces, sanitary napkins, newborn disposable diapers, powder or cornstarch, shirt or kimono, and a blanket. Gas pains aren't serious, so the day was spent picking tomatoes and canning tomato juice. At bedtime however, the contractions intensified and came from two to three minutes apart.

The water broke in a rush two hours before the birth, but it can come from thirty seconds to days before birth, and either in a trickle or a flood. Some women show some blood just before birth. There can be little or none, or a sizable amount. It varies from woman to woman.

Sundown's head emerged face down. Dee took the baby's head and gently turned it to allow her shoulders to rotate and follow out.

After Sundown was born, she cried to clear her nose and throat. If the baby doesn't cry by himself, use the well-known and effective slap on the butt.

The baby will be attached to the mother by the umbilical cord; the placenta or afterbirth is still in the uterus. The cord pulsates for ten to twenty minutes after birth, because it still carries blood to the baby. You should wait until the cord stops pulsating before you tie it off.

To tie it off, Dee took the cord in one hand and squeezed it shut near the mother. With the other hand she gently squeezed and pushed the blood back into Sundown. She tied the cord off about one inch from the baby with a boiled shoelace. The cord was also tied off about four inches from the first tie, and cut between the two ties, The ties have to be tight so blood can't seep out. We have seen the placenta come forth before the baby was tied off. There's no problem; the same procedure was followed.

The baby should be put to the breast immediately. This makes the baby feel warm and secure, and nursing stimulates the mother's uterus to contract and expel the placenta. The placenta should come forth within twenty to thirty minutes after birth.

After the first excitement of the birth has died down and everyone has themselves together, you will notice that the baby has a creamy substance on his skin. This is a natural lotion to moisturize his skin, and should be left on. Swab off the excess in the folds of the skin with cotton balls and baby oil, or if they are not available, a warm washcloth.

The first few days after birth, baby's bowel movements will be a tarry, sticky substance. It will be convenient to use disposable diapers or diaper liners until the bowel movements are normal. In the first weeks, he will also lose his cord, and his skin may peel or flake some. Keep him clean with a daily sponge bath, and use lotion on his skin to keep him moist.

For at least a week, you should massage your uterus every time you lie down. With your hand on your uterus, massage with a gentle, circular motion, and you can feel the uterus tighten into a ball. The tightening stops any bleeding in the uterus, and puts your belly back into shape. The baby's nursing has the same effect as the massage, so note the action in your uterus while nursing; then you will know if you are massaging correctly.

We were told that not putting silver nitrate in the baby's eyes was against the law. The Indiana 1971 code states that if parents object for religious reasons, they are exempt from this law. The only thing we were required to do was register Sundown's birth at the county courthouse.

The most important thing about childbirth is the preparation. Spiritual preparation is of prime importance if you are going to have your baby at home. We confessed for nine months that our baby was healthy and whole, and that the birth was normal and painless. Confession and the Word built our faith to the point that when the day came there was no fear, only happiness and rejoicing that the big moment had come. It gives so much peace to know that yours is a Jesus baby, and He's responsible for its health and well-being.

An added note: At this writing, Sundown Joy is fourteen months old, walking and talking like any baby. She was born at 3:22 A.M. amidst shrieks ("Look at all that hair! I never saw so much hair!") and gentle observances ("It's a Sundown, not an Eli"). As her birth gave so much pleasure, her life has given more. ". . . Joy comes in the morning" (Psalm 30:5). Sundown now has a two-week-old sister named Earlie Mist whom the Lord brought forth seven weeks early. Weighing in a 4 lbs. 4 oz., she is strong and healthy, another Jesus baby miracle. Hallelujah!

28-SEWING

We thought that in the end-times a good commercial treadle-type sewing machine would be valuable. Mac, who owns a shoe repair shop in Fort Wayne, showed us the 29-4 Singer, treadle-type, and told us that this was what we were looking for. A 29-4 Singer in good shape is worth $150.

A few days later, I was at Mr. Beasley's farm repair and blacksmith shop which is located a mile from us. I spotted a treadle that was covered up with a canvas in the corner, and like things "happen" for believers, it happened to be a 29-4 Singer. It was really in good shape. I didn't have the $150, and the devil was trying to tell me to tell him that it wasn't so good, because if I told Mr. Beasley what the machine was worth, that's what he'd want. The devil was really running me some games. The Lord put me under conviction about telling him exactly what the machine was worth, so I told Mr. Beasley I'd like to buy his sewing machine. He asked me what I thought it was worth. I told him it was worth $150, and I'd like to buy it for $50. Everybody laughed.

He said he had only paid $25 for it, and I was "getting took" if I paid him $50.

I said, "I think I'd better tell you again. If I put this on the truck and take it to Fort Wayne, I can sell it for $150. Your machine is worth $150."

Again, everybody laughed.

"You just pay me $50 whenever you can," he said, there's no hurry about it, just take the machine, and we'll see you!"

Praise the Lord!

Since then, we've been able to use the machine for repairing canvas, a harness for the horse, belts, shoes, and jackets. We're very pleased that the Lord gave us this sewing machine. With the abundant supply of thread and extra needles that Mac's Shoe Repair gave us, the machine has been able to help in cutting down repair costs. This is an area where we'll be able to help people later on.

29-LIGHTING, LIGHTS, CANDLES

When we talk to people about lighting in this self-sufficiency realm, they usually think of the wind generator, hydro-power, creek or river, or gasoline generator. All these things will give you light, but who are you going to buy your lightbulb from when you can't buy or sell? This eliminates most of the exotic types of self-sufficiency lighting.

Our situation here is going to depend upon kerosene lamps for a time. We intend to use whatever fuel oil we have left in our heating system. Fuel oil is definitely not kerosene, however, and will blacken the chimneys and smell. We had quite a search for pure kerosene that wound up in Amish-land in northern Indiana. The Amish run their refrigerators on refined, good quality, old-time kerosene. We only know of two places, one in Michigan and one in Pennsylvania, that still produce pure kerosene. We have small quantities now.

The next step we will be going into is candles. These will be made out of tallow, which is the fat substance that protects beef kidneys. This is a crunchy, crumbly tallow, and not fat. Some people have tried making candles out of refined animal fat (grease), but these candles are not firm, and they smoke. We made candles out of pure tallow. Eventually, when we get wax from our bees, we will be coating our tallow candles with three coats of beeswax. This is done to give the outside a firmer coating. This is an excellent quality candle.

The hardest part of candle-making is getting the wax to the exact temperature. For making pure beeswax candles, the wax can be heated to about 160°, but if you are making tallow candles, the wax must be lowered to 125° to 135°. I test the degree of heat with a candy thermometer.

I made a hand-dipper where I could straighten the wick on it and dip sixteen candles at a time. About every three to five minutes, dip the candles into the wax very slowly, so there won't be any bubbles. We went in and out too fast, and they really do bubble on the side. It's not just throw it in and dip it out. It is probably clearer to say: One, submerge the candles; two, hold it; three, pull it out. One, two, three, and then let it set for three to five minutes.

The first batch we tried, we used a commercial wick from the Wax Factory, a candle-making store. We used a lead-core wick and although it worked okay and burned very slowly, I feel the next time we will use a No. 3 or 4 wick that doesn't have a lead core. You can use anything like cotton string or thread. You could take apart old cloth and braid them into a wick. After the wick is braided, coat it with beeswax.

For you who live in the southern states, you can extract wax from the seed pods of a tree called a "tallow tree."

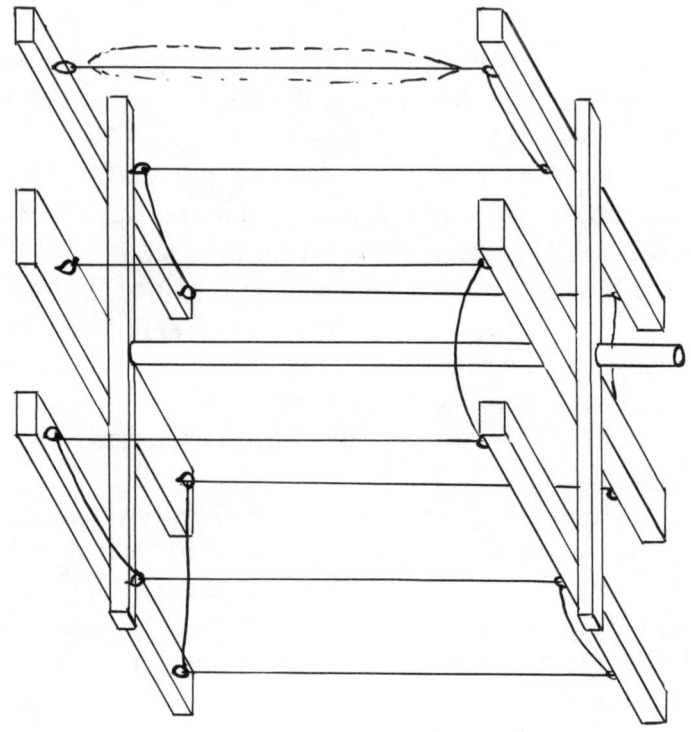

We read that in Bible times they had no candles as we know them. They burned a wick made of flax in a shallow bowl and used olive oil for fuel.

We also read that in the early United States, candles were of such great value that they were only used for reading the Bible. This really ministered to us, and that's what we'll be using our candles for, too. Of course, we'll also have light from our fireplace.

30-CABIN

In January of 1974, Danny came by. His brother had a condemned lake cottage that he wanted torn down. He offered to give us the lumber and $200 to tear the place down. Ray and Gary, "The Least of These" singing duo, were living with us at the time. They worked on it for a week, and got it completely torn down. Just before they were done, an old motorcycle friend of Mel's offered us the shed and a lot of lumber from a lumber yard he was remodeling into a craft mall. We thought it would be a good chance for Ray and Gary to witness as well as to perfect their newly acquired talents for remodeling. Before they were done with the job, Mike came by and asked if we would like the material from an old grain elevator. By this time we were wondering how in the world we were going to use all this lumber and tin roofing.

During the summer Dirk worked on pulling the nails out of the lumber, washing and stacking it. Anyone who came by for a few days had a good chance to learn the fascinating art of nail pulling and wood cutting. By September, we had a lot of neatly stacked, inventoried eight foot, ten foot, twelve foot and sixteen foot piles of wood all over the sideyard. The Lord had been dealing with Mel to build a cabin without electricity or power of any kind. The cabin would be another step toward self-sufficiency.

We bought the books *Wilderness Cabin* and *Shelter*. *Wilderness Cabin* has information on the most efficient sized cabin for heating, the same size Indiana pioneers used. *Shelter* has floor plans and "how to" information. We checked our inventory of lumber and figured out which cabin we could build.

We had some cement blocks, rescued from a burned-out building, that we used for the foundation. We bought some cement and got sand and gravel free from the local sand pit. We also bought some tar paper to cover our subflooring and keep the drafts down.

Between January and August, six different friends had given us material that we eventually used for the cabin. We were given a front door from a mobile home builder that our friend Benny had sitting in his garage. Old Mame, who ran Ma Black's Jesus Center, replaced a set of windows and gave the old ones to us. Her son, Orley, gave us a huge thermopane window. Vic gave us a window and floor registers from his dad's house that was about to be torn down. Tip gave us a big old sink.

After all these donations, we still were one door and two windows short, so we asked at the lumber yard if they had any odd-sized materials. Joe, who works there, was remodeling a house, and had exactly what we needed. He said we could have them for hauling the scrap material away. Hallelujah!

It took six weeks of steady work to frame and close in the cabin. The kitchen and living room area are sixteen feet by twenty-eight feet with an eight foot ceiling. The sleeping loft is twelve feet by twenty-eight feet and the ceiling goes from four feet to eight feet. Behind the sleeping loft is a storage area four feet by eleven feet. The front porch is screened in and is eight feet by eleven feet, and the back porch is enclosed and is four feet by eight feet.

Fireplace

We framed in a fireplace on the north wall, but it is yet to be built. We are doing a fireplace just for the romance and recreation, because a fireplace really isn't an efficient way to heat or cook.

The easiest way to get a fireplace effect with more efficient uses is to have a Franklin stove. We have one in our apartment at the Barn, and it's really been a blessing to us. We can grill on it, cook on it, and heat with it—a stove and furnace all in one.

You can install a Franklin stove if you have an existing chimney. Maybe you have one that's been paneled or plastered over. You can chip it out, plug your Franklin stove right into it, and be ready to go.

Once the cabin was framed in, we put the tin roof on and painted it with aluminum asphalt paint. Then we covered the sides with insulated sheathing, and nailed the flooring down.

Next we put the chimney in, and had to buy chimney blocks, flue liner, and a chimney cap.

Heating and Cooking

We wondered just what the Lord would have us do for a stove for heating and cooking. One day, two boys drove up to the Glory Barn with a Globe Maid wood-burning cook stove on the back of their pick-up truck. The stove was in perfect condition except for one place where the enamel had been chipped. We asked where they got it, and they said they had taken it out of an old house that was being torn down. They had taken it to a flea market, unloaded it (which you don't want to do unless you have four guys) and were offered $7.50 for it. They got upset, put it back on the truck, and stopped by our place. We had $23 at the time. We thought they probably wouldn't take that for it either, but offered them $20 anyway. They said, "Where do you want it?" So we will be cooking on an old wood range we bought for $20. Some of these stoves are worth $300 to $400 apiece. The Lord supplied that stove for us!

Make a note that when buying a cookstove, be sure that the grates are okay and the top is not warped from overheating. These stoves are not to have coal burned in them because it burns too hot.

The Lord had taken care of our cooking, but what was the way to go for our heating? We had looked around for some stoves, and they were all pretty high priced. Finally, we bought a kit from Fatsco in Benton Harbor, Michigan, that utilizes a 55-gallon drum. We took a drum, put fire bricks in the bottom, laid it in with sand, and put another barrel on top of it for a plenham, which is a heat exchanger. The smoke goes through the plenham, which can have pebbles or small rocks in it to hold more heat, and up the chimney. This really provides good heat for our cabin.

Steve started out with a gas furnace in his house. We supplemented that with a little Warm Morning stove. It was a wood and coal stove, but actually too small to burn anything but coal, so we kept looking for a bigger, better one. We obtained an Army Warm Morning stove that was a top loader and almost the size of a 55-gallon drum. You can really put a chunk of wood in it. Again, Jesus led us to it. We bought this one for $25 and it's probably worth $200. So, when you are trying to find things like this, don't forget who your Leader is. Get into some prayer before you start, and let the Lord guide you in setting up your whole program.

Water Supply (Smokehouse, sauna, shower)

We had heard that driving a well by hand is very difficult, and it's true. We erected a tripod, hooked a pulley around the top, attached a well-driving weight, and drove the pipe down. At the hardware, we got a driving screen, or driving point. Twenty-three feet, many blisters, and a lot of prayer later, Jesus manifested a fountain like He promises in Deuteronomy 8:7-8, and the water started gushing out the top of the pipe.

Our well is 150 feet downhill from the cabin. Of course, after we got the well, the first thing we thought about was that we'd really like to have a way to get this water up over the hill and into a storage tank. Since we are not using electricity, generators, or gas, that seemed impossible.

We have a friend from Tennessee who had been coming here to the fellowship quite a lot. While back working on the cabin, he said that what we needed was a ram pump.

Mel said, "Well, Bob, you're just not listening. We're not using any gasoline, generators, or anything like that. We don't have any electricity back here."

Bob said that a ram pump runs strictly on hydraulic power. It will take water out of one reservoir, put it through a two-inch pipe, into the ram pump, and pump it out a one-inch pipe. There is a place in Tennessee where two of these have been working for forty years, and they pump water 100 feet straight up the mountain. We told him somebody was playing a trick on him, because this really seemed impossible. We told him to check on it and let us know what he found out. He insisted his dad had looked at these pumps, and there were no wires. They really did run by hydraulic power.

Not too many days later, Mel picked up a "how-to-do-it" book, and there on the first pages was a picture of a ram pump. That really surprised him. The ram pump was used in the United States in the early 30s and even now a Chicago mail order house sells them to missionaries to pump water long distances in remote areas.

Now that we wanted one, where did we get one? Another friend, Ron, from New York, hadn't been here for a year, and came by asking what we were doing with the farm. We told him that Jesus had led us to build a refuge in the wilderness for the people in the end-times, and we were going totally self-sufficient.

"Wow! You don't want to do that!" he said. "I had a brother in New York that went self-sufficient. He was growing hogs, and the hog feed started costing a lot of money, so he prayed, and the Lord showed him to give the hogs to certain people."

We told him that wasn't self-sufficiency. We were talking about *total* self-sufficiency, and handed him this "how-to-do-it" book to explain. He opened it up, and turned right to the ram pump page.

"Oh, do you need one of these?" he asked.

Did we! He works at a chocolate company and their trucks came through La Paz, which is only sixty miles from the Barn. So he put the pump and some valves on a truck, and had it here within a week after he got back home.

If you are interested in buying a ram pump for yourself, here's an address: Rife Hydraulic Mfg. Co., Box 367, Millburn, New Jersey 07041.

That took care of our getting the water from the bottom of the hill to the top. Now we have to build a reservoir at the bottom of the hill, so that it will gravity-feed the pump. The pump pushes the water up the hill, into a storage area. Below the storage area, we'll be putting in a shower, and a line from there into the cabin.

The sauna, smokehouse, reservoir, shower combination will be approximately twelve feet by eight feet. The top of the sauna will be where we store our water. We will be storing it in five or six 55-gallon barrels, and drawing from there for a shower. We'll be enclosing these barrels with windows from an old house, and the sun will heat the water. We will put in a concave floor and drain for the shower.

In the winter time, we will have a coil that wraps around the stove in the sauna. The fire in the stove will heat the rocks and coil that are held in place by fencing. The hot water will travel up through the coil into the storage area by capillary action. The heat from the stove will rise into the storage barrels and heat the water.

We will put a T with two dampers into the smokestack of the sauna stove so that we can route cold smoke from it out the back of the sauna into an old refrigerator that has been converted into a smokehouse.

One of the things you cannot forget is to provide an

air supply for the stove. This can be done by running a pipe from under the stove to the outside. If this is not done, the fire will exhaust your air supply.

The Privy

There's only so much you can say about a privy. However, there are whole books written about them. I've seen double toilets; not two holes—double, one on top of another. There are toilets that are also used for composting that open up in the back. There are toilets used to produce methane gas, also.

A lot of people will tell you to watch your water supply so that your toilet is not above your well, and this is good advice. Our hole is seven feet deep and three feet square, so we won't ever have to move it. It's a little too deep. Four feet deep and three feet by three feet would be sufficient.

We recycled an old outside toilet that was manufactured in the 1930s. It has a concrete base with a lid, and a pipe in the back for cross-ventilation. We had to paint it, replace all the broken boards and put new hinges on the door. The roof was a little tattery, so we took it off and went exotic by putting a plastic sun roof on. We added an old Sears and Roebuck catalog, and it's complete!

Furnishings

We have most of the furnishings for the cabin. We have a metal ice box that we found in a junk shop. We traded an old gas stove for two bunk beds for the kids to sleep in. In the garage, we had an old kitchen cabinet that we stripped down and then stained. A friend gave us a big kitchen table, and from somewhere a dresser turned up for clothing. We have also been given two couches (one a fold-out bed), bedding, dishes, huge coffee pots, blankets, bedspreads, etc.

We are now waiting on the Lord for the siding and insulation, and our cabin will be done.

The Lord continues to take care of what we need. One day when we were in Fort Wayne, Mac from Mac's Shoe Repair said he wanted to get rid of an above-ground swimming pool and a large shed. He wanted them moved so he could use the room to plant a garden (good idea!). He said we could have them if we'd take them. We moved the pool and it had a lot of good two-by-fours and plywood. (The shed was ten feet by sixteen feet.)

Instead of tearing it apart, Mike offered to bring a fifth wheel lo-boy and we backed up along the side of the shed, put come-alongs on it, tipped it onto the lo-boy, and away we went. We took it all the way to the Barn, and that's about fifty miles. We set the shed up, and found it had loosened some in the transporting. Jesus sent Dick, a drafting engineer on his way to Oregon, to engineer corner and cross-bracing in the shed. He also built a good-size sleeping loft in the tall end of it and a tool and paint storage area so that it is beginning to look like the "Northstar" that we read about in *Shelter*. Sally, a sister from the hardware store gave us a gas cooking range and oil stove, so we can use the shed as temporary housing. Later we intend to pull it to our cabin to be used as a goat shed, pigeon fly, or chicken coop.

We put it on runners so we can move it easily. Any kind of shed can really be useful, so if someone wants to get rid of one, take it!

Last week we were given another cabin. This is a regular pioneer style log cabin eighteen feet by twenty-two feet. We will use some of the siding they had on it to panel our cabin. This cabin will be set up for Steve and Dee near the Barn. As we said, the Lord continues to meet our needs!

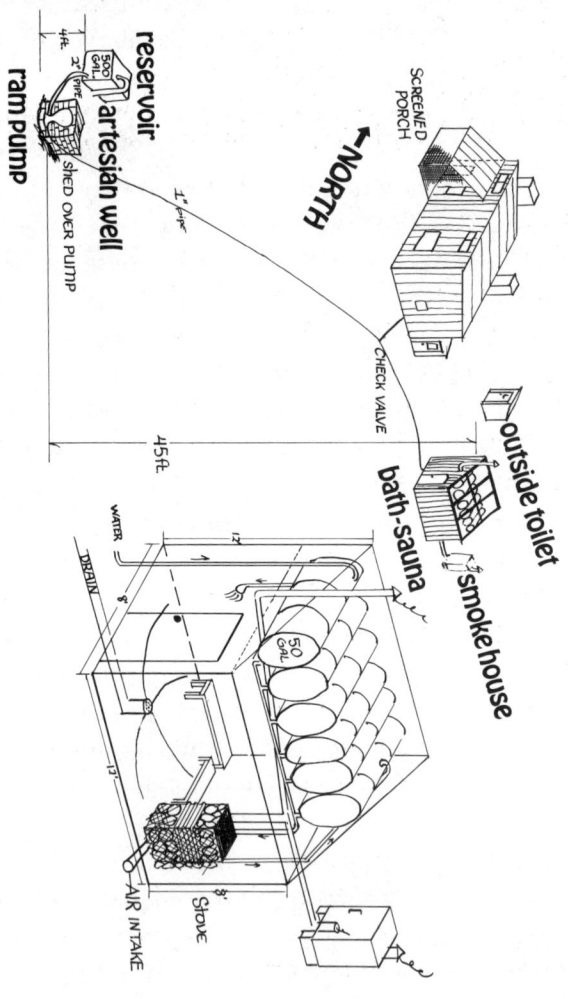

IN CONCLUSION

In the Midwest, western Kentucky, Illinois, Kansas, Iowa, and Missouri, an Electronic Fund Transfer System is now being set up. This consists of a $40 million computer set up at the bank, with smaller computers in the stores. The computer transfers the money from your account in the bank to the store. The same thing applies to your employment. The money from where you work will go directly to the bank, then you can go to the store, and everything will be transferred by the computer. This is the beginning of a one monetary system. The computer will be activated by a plastic laminated credit card-like card. What if someone loses his card? The program they've decided to use is to put an invisible tattoo on your forehead or your hand by a laser beam that can't be felt or seen with the naked eye, but is as permanent as fingerprints. You'll just walk up to the computer and the computer will record the number off your hand or forehead and do all the business.

The Lord says, "And the third angel followed them saying with a loud voice, "If any man worship the beast and his image, and receive his mark in his forehead or on his hand, the same shall drink of the wine of the wrath of God . . . and he shall be tormented with fire and brimstone" (Rev. 14:9-10).

This time is very close. We wish we knew exactly when, but the Lord says, "But of that day and that hour, knoweth no man, no, not the angels which are in heaven, neither the Son, but the Father" (Mark 13:13).

There has been a prophecy from our Body that was really anointed and in the Spirit. The prophecy said that whatever we do, we should do in great haste.

If somebody's talking to you about going self-sufficient, and you had to buy everything that you need, I would say you would need $35 to $40 thousand to get everything functioning. This kind of money has not been available to us.

The Lord has chosen to bring us materials to recycle. He has made us become resourceful, and given us talents that we didn't know we had. In other words, He puts our faith to the test. You know, He has made important to us the fact that faith is good, but faith without ever being tried, without works, is dead. I'm sure you've heard that many times before. He won't build a refuge in the end-times unless He is trying our faith, putting us to a test. He is definitely wanting us to put our trust in Him. We never want to lose sight of this. (It's God, and it's Jesus.) This is the way the thing is going to be run, this is how it has to be set up. We want to be grounded and founded on the Rock. If you intend to do something like we're suggesting in *Woman in the Wilderness*, and attack a program without prayer, and without the Lord in it, it just won't stand. We advise you to seek the Lord's face, and pray for Him to guide you.

We all agree that Jesus is to return soon, so whatever you do, do with great haste, also.

BIBLIOGRAPHY

Ball Blue Book. Ball Corporation, Muncie, Indiana 47302. $.50.

Cookbooks such as *Old Virginia, Searchlight,* and *White House* are out of print, but may be found at flea markets, grandmother's house, and attics.

Cumberland Gap General Store, Dept. MN, Route 3, Box 479, Crossville, Tennessee 38555. $3.00

Dairy Goat Journal. Box 1908 OG, Scottsdale, Arizona 85252. $5.00 per year subscription.

Encyclopedia of Organic Gardening and Farming. Order from Organic Gardening and Farming, Rodale Press, Inc., Book Division, Emmaus, Pennsylvania 10849. *Encyclopedia*, $14.95. *Organic Gardening*, $6.85 per year subscription.

Foxfire. Mother's General Store. #1, $3.95; #2, $4.50; #3, $.95.

Gay, Larry. *Heating With Wood.* Charlotte, Vermont: (05455) Gardening Publishing. $3.50

Herter, George Leonard. *Professional Guide's Manual.* Waseca, Minnesota: Herter. Contains hunting and trapping tips, information about knives, boating, camping, cooking venison, etc. $.50; larger, $2.50.

Hertzberd, Ruth; Beatrice Vaughn; and Greene, Janet. *Putting Foods By.* Mother's General Store, $4.95.

How to Keep Bees and Sell Honey. Walter T. Kelley Co., Clarkson, Kentucky 42726.

Kains, M. G. *Five Acres and Independence.* Mother's General Store. About small farm management. $2.50.

133

Langer, Richard. *Grow It.* Mother's General Store. $8.95.

Mother Earth News. Mother's General Store, Box 506, Flat Rock, North Carolina 28731. Mother Earth Subscription, $10 per year. Mother's General Store catalog, $.50

Olson, Larry Dean. *Outdoor Survival Skills.* Available at local bookstores. $3.95.

Rutstrum, Calvin. *Wilderness Cabin.* Collier Books, 866 Third Avenue, New York, New York 10022. $1.95.

Shelter. Shelter Publications. Mother's General Store. Good building ideas.

Stocking Up. Rodale Press. $8.95.